counter
intuitive

what 4 million teenagers wish we knew

(bite-sized wisdom 4 parents and teachers)

tyler durman

BSWisdom
Books

Counterintuitive
BSWisdom Books / February 2015

Published by BSWisdom Books
Laguna Beach, California

Cover Design by Jason Kleist
Book Layout Design by Todd Ford
Interior Artwork by Jenna Miller (19 years old)

Printed in La Vergne, Tennessee, in the United States of America

February 2015 ISBN 9780-9861-9735-2

TABLE OF CONTENTS

For Ken & Jessie Durman

01

They Will Run Somewhere

The ground was angled and dusty. As I walked with him down the path I smiled because this wasn't what I'd expected. No palms. No springs. I'd been fooled by the name.

"We'd love you to come speak at our school this August."

He wasn't what I'd expected either. When he called, his raspy voice brought to mind the image of a young Clint Eastwood from one of those old cowboy movies.

"Our students need to learn how to treat each other." His words squeezed past dusty vocal cords. "I'm trying to teach them to look beyond their differences and take care of each other."

Clint Eastwood with a compassionate heart. I liked him for that, so I told him I'd come.

Now, as I followed his round little body down the hill to the football stadium, I could see the only thing he had in common with a cowboy was his need for a hat. The sun had reached through his thinning hair to do its damaging work.

As we walked, I was unaware of what would be waiting for me later, as I went back up that same path alone.

"It's a bit hot, but us desert folk are used to it."

A bit hot? According to the car radio it was 108 degrees. Even Satan wouldn't come near this place in August. He'd scheduled the program to be outside because it was the only place he could fit all his students at once. There was no shade or breeze, so I smiled politely as I watched 1,700 high school students sizzle their way onto the concrete seats.

These were tough kids, many of them in gangs, but the principal was able to quiet them to introduce me. When I stood to speak 3,400 eyes begged, "Mister, please don't take the entire hour. It's already been three whole minutes. I'm done on this side, flip me over."

From my perspective the minutes trickled past, and yet despite the temperature, the students stayed engaged throughout. Some were even moved to tears, and when the final applause came it was loud and sincere.

Well okay, the tears may have been sweat, and the applause because I'd finally shut up – but either way, it was great to be done.

After a wet hug from my non-cowboy, his eyes moist with gratitude, I headed for the ergonomic comforts of my rental car. As I walked, I held my keys in my hand and kept my eyes to the ground so no one would slow my escape.

*   *   *

I was halfway up the hill when I heard her voice. She said seven words I hoped were meant for someone else, but when I glanced back she was following me, and she was alone.

"There's something I need to tell you."

I squeezed out a smile and invited her to join me in the shade of a nearby tree where the temperature was only ninety-nine.

That's when I saw something in her expression I'd missed at

first. Her eyes were a deep well filled with the kind of sorrow that's only fit for someone who's been alive much longer, and been worn down by the weight of extensive and permanent heartache. I found myself teetering there on the edge of her sadness, trying not to fall in.

*   *   *

Normally after I speak, students come up to say hi, some ask if we can talk, and invariably an extraordinary thing happens – they tell me things they've never told anyone before.

I think they feel they can do this because I don't know their friends, parents or teachers, and they realize after we're done talking I'll be flying out of town. This means their secrets are safe, so sometimes they'll wait an hour or more for their turn to confess or confide.

I've had thousands of these conversations, and their raw honesty gives me a glimpse into a private world few adults ever see. They teach me things about teenagers I never learned in a book, or as a teacher, or by sitting across from a student in the formal setting of a counseling office.

Standing there now, looking into this girl's eyes, I readied myself because I had the feeling I was about to be invited into someplace dark.

I'd been hoping everyone would run toward the air-conditioned buildings because the only conversation I wanted was with a 7-Eleven clerk about a Big Gulp. But now, those thoughts were gone as I leaned against the tree for support.

Her eyes were down and she rocked just slightly. I could tell she wasn't used to letting anyone inside.

"What's your name?"

"Moema." Her voice was quiet, as if apologizing.

"That's pretty. I've never heard that name before"

She looked up. "It's Native American."

"Do you know what it means?"

"Sweet One." And I could tell she was.

For just a second, while she defined her name, a hint of light pulsed through her countenance. It was a sharp contrast to the shades of black she was wrapped in – from her baggy clothes to her dyed hair and overdone makeup.

She asked if she could tell me something she'd never told anyone. A secret she'd kept since she was six. Over half her life.

I nodded and slipped my keys into a pocket, as she began to turn hers in the door of her past. I could see she was fumbling with the lock.

"I've wanted to tell my mom a thousand times, but I never could."

Her breath stuttered, and the weight of all those moments came together in this one with a suddenness that startled me. There was a loud sob and she collapsed forward, falling into me.

She shook as she wept.

Terrified of rejection, her sixteen years had not yet taught her real safety is only possible when we come out of hiding.

After a brief moment I stood her up, smiled and said, "Keep going."

She nodded, took a deep wet breath, gathered herself and went on.

Her secret was born on the angled ground of another hill, not far from where we stood. It had been a Saturday, following a rare and long rain. The skies had drained themselves with such passion that streams had become rivers and the aqueducts, torrents. When the sun at last pushed back the clouds, their babysitter took Moema and her little brother outside for some fun.

Their play led the four- and six-year-old along the side of an aqueduct that was screaming its course nearby. There on the slope, enveloped by the sound of the water, Moema and her little brother began throwing rocks and sticks. They were delighted with their new plaything, unaware it was waiting to devour any prey it could touch.

The water had cast some bait within reach. Both kids saw it. It was a stick. Just a stick. But in the eyes of the children, it was perfect.

As they ran for it, the sound of the torrent drowned out their giggles – and the screams of their sitter. At precisely the same moment they lunged, grasped, and fell. Moema onto the ground, her little brother into the water, where he was swallowed whole and vanished. She screamed, stood, turned. The blur of the sitter's dive caught the corner of her eye. And then she was alone.

She would never see either of them again.

And that was it. Her secret was born at the death of her brother. She believed she was the killer, not the water; that she was the murderer, not the mistake.

She didn't know what to do. Jump in? Scream? Run? She was only six. Only 6. So she screamed. No one came and she was still alone. Eventually the little dazed girl stumbled back to the street, led by the sound of her anguish.

Her eyes were wild with fear when a car stopped. There was a nice man. A police siren. An ambulance. Faces. Questions. More faces. More questions. But none were the face of her little brother. When would he come home? He won't? Never?

Never.

After the faces disappeared, her questions continued and became the private refrain that welcomed her to each emptier day.

"I was so scared, Tyler." Her voice desperate now. "I didn't want my mom to hate me. I didn't want to go to jail, so I lied and said he'd fallen in by himself!"

She rocked her head back and wailed, "I killed my little brother!"

She fell into me again, her body one big tremble.

I stood there with her shudders pressing into me, searching for something to say. Nothing came. All I knew was no one could be strong enough to carry such weight alone.

I can't say how long it was before she stepped back and stood on her own, but when she did her eyes were vacant. She was spent and looked like a hollow replica of herself.

Her life had been dominated by lies: Her mother's weeping, her fault. Her parents' divorce, her fault. Her dad's alcoholism, her fault.

Like some dying flower she had closed in on herself, solitary confinement her punishment. Self-loathing and guilt had led to depression and continual thoughts of suicide. She only stayed alive, she said, to save her mom from more pain.

"I wish I could have told her everything a long time ago."

She paused.

"I know she loves me, but she likes to pretend she's perfect, so she's the last person I can talk to."

And there it was, a lesson I've heard dozens of times, and in stories far less dramatic than Moema's. Like the rest of us, *teenagers need a safe place to run when they fail. They will run somewhere, and the way the adults in their lives respond to failure will determine whether they run to us or away from us.*

*   *   *

I felt compassion for Moema's mom because of all she'd been through. After losing her little boy, she'd lost her marriage. And now, standing there in the shadow of that tree, I could see she was losing her daughter as well.

Hiding her weaknesses by pretending to be perfect in front of Moema must have felt right to her. But her intuition was misleading her, because pretending doesn't bring credibility, it creates distance. In fact, her imperfections may have been her most powerful tool to create intimacy with her daughter.

It's not that she should have confessed all the darkest things from her past, but her unwillingness to be real in the moment by saying things like "I'm sorry" or "I blew it and need you to forgive me" had made her unapproachable.

She didn't realize that *by pretending to be perfect, she was raising her daughter under a kind of curse.* She was teaching Moema that mistakes should be hidden, so home was the last place Moema could be real and feel safe at the same time. That environment had taught Moema her value was based on her performance, so she lived with the fear of being found out.

On the other hand, if Moema's mom had allowed her daughter to watch as she dealt openly with her own weaknesses, she would have given Moema a gift. It would have shown her that failure isn't final, that mistakes don't decrease our worth, and that intimacy is possible even with all our flaws.

*   *   *

Moema and I stayed in the shadow of that tree for about fifteen minutes, and she told me another reason her mom hadn't been a safe place for her.

"There's been a few times I was about to tell her everything, but then she'd freak out over something small, which she does pretty much every time I do anything wrong."

I hear this a lot, and think it's because as adults, we want to save kids from the big painful lessons of life, so we try to head them off by coming down extra hard on the smaller things.

So when we find the hidden *Sports Illustrated Swimsuit Issue* under our son's mattress, we react as though he's just accepted an internship with Hugh Heffner. Or when our daughter mentions she's thinking about putting a purple streak in her hair, we react as if she just got the Harley Davidson logo tattooed across the front of her neck.

Our trigger might be nutrition, neatness, being on time, or how they dress, which all have importance, but they're not the same thing as belligerence or stealing or substance abuse or disrespect, and we shouldn't react as if they are. When we do, our lectures become white noise and we become the last place they'll go to confide, heal or find wisdom.

And so, because she couldn't run to her mom, she'd chosen to run away from everyone else. She had no sleepovers, no friends, no dates. Just hollow weeks spent alone in her room. Her iPod her armor. Her black clothes her mourning.

It's a horrible thing to live with a secret kept out of fear or shame, and hers had owned her since that day at the aqueduct.

But not anymore.

I was there and got to listen as the lonely six-year-old reached out her teenage hand and dragged the ugly thing into the open.

And on that dusty ground, on that new hill, it finally met its match. I watched it squirm. Witnessed its last twitch. And its death was marvelous.

When I told her she hadn't caused her brother's death, she reacted like a bird that's never known freedom, and sits at the open door of its cage in hesitation and disbelief.

I had to repeat it in several ways before it began to sink in. But when it did, for the first time, Moema learned she was not to blame. Her sitter had made the tragic mistake. Inertia and gravity had taken her brother and it wasn't her fault. She'd only been six. A little first-grader. She was innocent then, and she was innocent now.

Innocent?

Innocent.

What a beautiful word.

Moema. Sweet one. Set free.

The tears she cried now were different. They were liquid relief.

We walked and talked for a while, and I encouraged her to call home, saying even though her mom had made mistakes, it wasn't too late for a new start. She said she would, so we went inside and used the school phone.

"It's me. I'm in the office. Can you come get me? ... I'll tell you when you get here, but don't worry, it's not bad."

She asked if I'd be with her when she told her mom, so we waited just inside the school doors. The principal saw us and his round face broke into a smile. As he walked toward us I suggested she should tell him too, and with that she let someone else know the truth, and once again, discovered she was safe.

He was wise and knew he didn't need to say many words.

"If you ever need to talk, I'm here."

Just then her mom pulled up, and Moema took a deep breath. She invited him to join us, and he said he would in a minute, so the two of us sprinted through the heat and burst into the car. Her into the front, and me into the back.

I'd been so wrapped up in everything it hadn't dawned on me what this moment would be like for her mom, as some six-foot-six old guy exploded through the back door and slid to a stop on the seat directly behind her.

Sometimes I am very dumb.

The fear that sprang across her face as she spun toward me snapped me into reality, and I tried to ease her anxiety with a lame joke about not being a carjacker.

A tap on the window saved me. It was the principal, and he did what intelligent humans do. He introduced himself and asked if he could take a seat inside.

"Moema's got something great to tell you, and I didn't want to miss it, if that's okay."

He and I sat quietly in the back as Moema began her story.

Her mom's eyes filled as she listened, her own pain seeping down her cheeks. And before Moema could finish, she grabbed her daughter to her chest and said, "It wasn't your fault. I'm so sorry! It wasn't your fault!"

Watching it unfold was like witnessing a sixteen-year-old being born all over again. Only this time, instead of a doctor, Clint's twin was there to help the birth along. His eyes were moist again as he poured love on that little family like it was his last act before entering the O.K. Corral.

When the time came for me to leave, he walked me out and gave me another wet hug before I got into my car.

"Don't worry about Moema or her mom. We'll stay involved."

I told him I was grateful, and as I bent into the car asked, "Could you do me a favor?"

He nodded, "Sure! Anything."

I closed the door and rolled the window down. "Would you mind saying, 'Do you feel lucky? Well, do ya, punk?'"

He laughed, "Yeah, I get that a lot."

I clicked on the A/C, "You should come visit us at the beach sometime, escape all this heat."

"What heat?"

"I'm serious, come down, or even use the house when we're away. You'd have to pick up poop when you walk our two golden retrievers, but you should be used to that kind of thing given your job."

He laughed again. "Feels like that some days, but not today."

I thanked him again for his help with Moema, and he said she was a brave girl.

I agreed, and my heart was full as I drove away in search of some palms and springs.

02

They're Not Done On The Inside

I'm looking out the bay window of a faculty-club apartment at the University of California in Santa Barbara. The Pacific Ocean sits just beyond the pool, and both their surfaces are calm and sparkling with sunlight. There's an old guy sunning on a beach chair with skin the color and texture of my wallet, and I'm wondering if he's the Dermatology professor.

For each of the past twenty summers I've come here to speak to almost 2000 high school student leaders from Orange County who are, coincidentally, also quite tan.

The kids at this event are pretty impressive, the cream that's risen to the top of their communities. I enjoy being around them because they're articulate, self-motivated, and use deodorant. They know more about technology, math and politics than I ever will, and many of them are more mature than I am, as evidenced by the fact they no longer watch SpongeBob.

When I was in school I would never have been a part of this elite group, because like most other teenage boys in my town, I spent most my time kicking a soccer ball or hiding in my room to peek at indigenous women in the pages of National Geographic.

Because these leaders are exceptional, in the early years I made the mistake of assuming they were as adult as I was. But then, as I listened to the private stories they shared with me, *I discovered even the most impressive teenagers still have powerful and lingering childhood needs lurking below the surface.*

In this way, they're a lot like barbecue chicken. Just because they look done on the outside doesn't mean they're done on the inside.

*   *   *

I met Josiah last summer at this conference and a few months later sat alone with him in the bleachers at his school. At seventeen, he'd been elected by 2,200 students to be their vice president. When he asked if we could talk I noticed the color of his leadership T-shirt highlighting the dime sized birthmark on his right cheek. They were both a muted red.

He explained he splits his time between his divorced parents' homes. "But that's not what I want to talk about; I'm fine with all that. There's just something I wanted to ask."

We were sitting shoulder to shoulder and he was looking down at his hands, the one worrying over the knuckles of the other.

"Here's the thing."

He paused, then pushed the words past the lump in his throat.

"My dad doesn't love me."

The words came with a sob; his eyes filled but he recovered quickly, as if he'd had lots of practice. A tear escaped and dripped from his nose just before his hand got there to wipe it.

"It's obvious he doesn't care about me because he lets me get away with pretty much everything. He buys me anything I want, but never gets upset or yells when I do stuff I shouldn't."

His eyes were full again. He dabbed them with the sleeves of his T-shirt, and his birthmark seemed to flush a deeper red.

"My friends all talk about how strict their parents are, and how cool it would be to have what I have, but I..."

His words dropped off. There was another stuttered breath and then, "It just feels like he's not really there for me, you know?"

I asked him to tell me more, and listened till he was talked out. The heart of it was that his dad treated him more like a roommate than a son, like they were equals, and he hated it.

When he was done, he glanced at me for the first time since we'd sat, and asked his question. "Is there something wrong with me for feeling all this? Does it mean I'm weak or something?"

Where a young woman needs to feel cherished, a young man needs to feel strong.

"Everything you're feeling is normal, and it definitely doesn't mean you're weak."

I asked if he'd ever told his dad how he felt, and he said he'd tried but it hadn't helped. "He's pretty big on us being friends. Says my grandpa was never around so he just wants us to be close. I don't know if he could ever understand what I'm feeling. I don't even understand it."

I explained that every teenager who's ever confided in me needed more from the adults in their life than friendship. "It's normal to want your dad to be more than an equal, so you know he's stronger than you, and there to guide and discipline and protect you. Those are normal needs. And they don't make you weak."

He said he hadn't thought of it like that, and it was a relief to hear.

"I bet if you ever have kids you're going to be a pretty amazing dad. I think the pain you're feeling now will help you then. Pain can be good in that way."

"Thanks. I hope so."

"Your dad may never understand what you need, but I bet there're other adults you respect, and it's not a bad thing to lean on them when you need to."

He nodded, "There's a couple people I could talk to."

"And I bet they don't just act like friends all the time."

He smiled. "No, they're both actually pretty tough teachers."

We spoke for a few more minutes, and before he left I said, "You know how to reach me, so keep me posted, okay?"

He said he would and thanked me again.

As I watched him walk across the gym and disappear into the hall, I was humbled because our conversation had reminded me of the times my mindset had been the same as his dad's. Times I'd been sincere and followed my intuition, only to discover later how wrong I'd been. Thinking of Josiah now helps me remember that it's possible to be sincere and wrong at the same time, and that a lot of what it takes to love a teenager well is completely counterintuitive.

When Josiah said, "It just feels like he's not really there for me," he was describing a raw longing to have a dad who wouldn't let him "get away with everything."

So why would any teenager say they want more discipline, when it seems all they talk about is wanting more freedom? The answer lies beneath the surface. At a deep level Josiah was aware he wasn't done on the inside. He was in touch with the primal need all teenagers have, to know there's someone over him. Someone he could trust to provide safety and guidance.

He wasn't weak; he just wasn't ready for total freedom and could sense it. *He equated the level of his father's love with his dad's willingness to relate to him like a parent and not a peer.*

I want to show you something that'll clarify why I say this with such confidence. For just a moment, let's look back to when Josiah, or any child, turned two. If we could climb into a two-year-old's onesie and see things through the child's eyes, we'd understand them a lot better after they reach puberty.

*   *   *

Two-year-olds shed light on teenagers.

You've lived for twenty-four months, seen two summers, can remember only one, and overall things have been pretty great.

You discovered early on that the universe had given you a couple of servants to help you along the way. You know this because even in the middle of the night when you scream, one of them always appears above your crib – usually the one with more hair. You've noticed that when you spit, urinate or even defecate on them, they still coo at you, even while wiping your royal butt.

Now that's loyalty.

All this has taught you that you are the center of the world.

Sometimes, because of their gratitude, one of your servants will put you in a portable little throne and wheel you around in public just so other big people can get down on one knee and attempt to evoke a smile from your highness.

You assume that your servants derive their sole meaning in life from making you happy. What you don't know is that even though they love you, sometimes they don't like you, and privately long for the day when you go to college. But in spite of this, they keep serving you, because if they don't, you will actually die. And that would be bad because the authorities know they have you.

Lately, though, you've begun to suspect that their loyalty is waning.

They used to feed you; now they tell you to hold your own spoon. They used to pick you up when you cried; now they just tell you to stop. And they used to change your diaper, but now they're trying to get you to use the potty, and you think, "I liked it better when you wiped my butt!"

Feeding and wiping and holding have all been bonding experiences, so now that your parents are less willing to do them, you feel like they're withdrawing. This scares you because you're beginning to recognize just how much you need them.

Add to this that your brain has now developed to the point that you are aware of your "separateness." In the early days, as a newborn, you believed that all things were connected to and an extension of yourself. In this way, you were a lot like the Kardashians.

But now you are realizing that "Mommy and me are separate human beings" and that "I am not my daddy, and my daddy is not me." This makes you feel even more vulnerable, and leads to what psychologists call separation anxiety.

So in order to feel more secure you challenge the strength of your parents to find reassurance that they are indeed still there for you.

You think, "I'm mad at you for all this change, so I'm going to keep throwing this Sippy-cup on the floor, no matter what you say."

Sometimes when you do this, or other things like it, your parents get upset and firmly tell you to stop. But other times they don't seem to care or act distracted, so you never know where you stand. The inconsistency makes your life a frantic kind of existence.

The less safe you feel, the more you need to test.

Your defiant behavior isn't a calculated personal attack against them or proof that you're demon possessed, but is rather the expression of how much you need to feel secure in your changing world.

Things begin to settle down after a year or so, as you adjust to the new normal.

*   *   *

What it feels like to be a teenager.

If an optometrist has ever given you a prescription, then you understand some of what it feels like when children go through puberty and their brain experiences one of its most dramatic growth spurts.

When I went to pick up my first pair of glasses, the doctor brought me outside and said, "Watching people put them on for the first time is why I do what I do."

I thought it was maybe for the three hundred bucks he'd put on my credit card. But what a surprise! I hadn't the slightest idea what I'd been missing.

I looked up and could see thousands of individual leaves on the trees, and the clouds were full of shadows and textures. Things were more detailed and beautiful.

But when I got home and looked in the mirror I recoiled. I was used to seeing myself through a soft blur that hid my imperfections.

"Could this be?" I wondered. "Is it possible that the pores on my face are actually that big? I could lose my keys in there. Have I really been walking around like this and nobody's loved me enough to suggest an esthetician? And holy crap, the skin around my eyes looks even *worse* than my wallet. I'm going to be alone forever!"

It took weeks to recover.

Before puberty, your life was like mine before glasses. There weren't as many details. Things were uncomplicated and comfortable. There was good and there was bad, with few shades of gray (nowhere near fifty).

"Is he a good guy, or a bad guy, Mommy?"

There wasn't much ethical nuance, textured meaning, or moral ambiguity.

But then as your brain suddenly grows, you discover intellectual abilities you've never known. You now have a greater power for conceptual and abstract reasoning, and are much more sensitive to nuance, analysis and critical thinking. In this way, you are definitely not like the Kardashians.

You literally have a new brain, and your abilities to think, reason and question are exhilarating. It's exciting to be on par with the adults around you, and it feels like you're in the game for the first time.

It brings pleasure to debate (or even argue) because it's like playing with a new toy, so you begin to form opinions on everything. At school you're being praised for thinking critically, and around the house, your new confidence causes you to question the things you've always taken at face value.

You feel powerful.

And yet there's also an unsettling downside. You can now see the large pores and wrinkles on life's face.

Your social world has become trickier to navigate. Your earlier friendships were built more on convenience than connection, but now you long for something deeper, which brings with it the fear of rejection.

For the first time you have the unhappy ability to read changing moods and disapproving looks in the subtle face expressions of those around you. This makes school a minefield. You're being judged by new and more complicated criteria, and everyone seems to be shifting alliances for self-preservation.

You feel less safe.

You are now very aware that there are boobs in the world, which is great if you're growing them and not so great if you aren't, and even worse if you're a boy and they're the only thing you can think about.

For others, there's something about boobs that's no laughing matter. If you happen to be a boy who's not attracted to girls because you're gay or think you might be, then you know you're one of the favorite targets of the bullies who roam the halls. The same is true if you're a girl who's attracted to girls. These new, postpuberty bullies are more relentless and cruel to your face, and even worse on-line, and you've watched them fixate on their victims in the same way wolves pursue and take down prey. If you haven't yet found the courage to be honest about who you are, you pretend to be something you're not while you carry the terrifying dread that at any moment you might be discovered.

But regardless of who you are, guy or girl, gay or straight, full figured or not, you know that pretending is a lonely way to live. With so much change pushing and pulling within you, it's hard to know who you are exactly, so you wear the identity that seems safest. You might find yourself wearing a different one around your peers than you do at home, or at church, or in the other circles you enter.

You want to be valued for who you are, but figuring out who that is feels daunting.

Of all the challenges in your new complicated life, there's a single awareness that bursts in upon you with such force it rocks the foundation of everything that's ever made you secure. You're shaken when it occurs to you for the first time that the key adults in your life are flawed and fragile.

John Steinbeck says it this way:

"When a child first catches adults out – when it first walks into his grave little head that adults do not have divine intelligence, that their judgments are not always wise, their thinking true, their sentences just – his world falls into a panic desolation. The gods are fallen and all safety gone. And there is one sure thing about the fall of gods: they do not fall a little; they crash and shatter or sink deeply into green muck. It is a tedious job to build them up again; they never quite shine. The child's world is never quite whole again. It is an aching kind of growing."

(East of Eden. 1952, p. 19-20)

And there it is: "The gods are fallen and all safety is gone," and it feels like betrayal.

You've always had a fallback position, but now the credibility of the adults around you has been diluted. You feel like a soldier on the frontlines who's just turned to discover he's alone.

Add to all this the confusion of romance, the power of your sex drive, the awkwardness of your growing body, your understanding of the instability of the world, the threat of terrorism, the pressures of social media, of sexting, of cyber bullying, of success, of trying to get or stay thin, and a familiar pattern emerges that harkens back to when you were two. *You feel vulnerable,* but this time the prices are higher, the risks greater, and the testing more powerful.

And so, like Josiah, because you're not done on the inside, you look to the behavior of the adults in your life to provide reassurance that everything is going to be okay. When the inner conflict between your desire for independence and your need to feel safe confuses them, you feel more fear, which can lead to anger and a new kind of testing.

*   *   *

It was July, and iPhone Girl was spitting *her* anger everywhere...

03

They Don't Test to Win

I'm at the beach and she's about twelve feet across the sand from where I'm sitting. The tantrum she just threw was louder than the waves and full of such hostility and practiced disrespect, it's clear this wasn't a one-time thing.

She punctuated her disgust by jamming her iPhone ear buds back into her head, stomping a few yards away, and snapping open her beach chair.

Her back is facing her parents now, and she's tapping the toes of her left foot against the tension in the air.

Poor thing. About fourteen years old and forced to sit in the tropical sun, on a white beach that stretches from the crystal water right up to the French doors of her family's $500-per-night condo. And to make things worse, it's about noon here in Kauai, and her dad won't, like, stop offering to buy her a $15 cheeseburger. Jeez!

He's such a jerk! How does he expect her stomach to stay flat if he keeps offering food?

A moment ago, her yelling startled everyone within earshot. The arteries in her neck protruded as she emphasized each word with a forceful thrust of her head right in her mom's face.

"Well tell him to get off my back, and both of you quit bugging me!"

Her parents stood there and watched her stomp away and slam her chair down. They glanced at each other with simultaneous sighs, and pretended to be busy with their own chairs. As Dad sat, Mom threw furtive glances around the beach while the rest of us pretended not to stare.

There's more than just humidity hanging in the air now. The conflict has added an awkward heaviness that seems to be draped over these parents' shoulders like a wet towel.

In a few moments, of course, the trade winds will blow most of the tension out to sea and the rest of us will go back to our magazines, naps and novels. But I suspect for this family, some of it will lurk, waiting for the inevitable moment when the daughter's resentment is triggered again.

Thin ice is a terrible way to live.

Watching people on family vacation has always felt to me like going to the zoo. You get to observe them huddled in close-knit groups, outside their natural habitat, and it's amazing how often they act like chimps that fling poo at each other.

I've seen it a lot because I used to live about five minutes from where I'm sitting. My weeks were full of surfing then, and my stomach was full of fresh fruit and ahi tuna. No cheeseburgers for me. I was a local. Tan. Relaxed. In shape.

But now, just thirty-six months after moving to the mainland, I'm the one in the zoo. I'm pale, scrawny, and smell like the other tourists because of the lotion slathered on my see-through skin. All I can think about is that cheeseburger the dad mentioned, and I want to yell across the sand that I'll take him up on his offer myself.

But I won't, because from here I can see that his face is still red and it has nothing to do with the sun.

iPhone girl's chair is rocking just slightly now. The song must have changed and she's tapping out the rhythm of her independence with a bit more fervor as she scrolls through twitter.

For their part, her parents have buried their feet in the sand. Mom is looking at a magazine while Dad reads the book *Odd Thomas* by Dean Koontz. It happens to be one of my favorite novels because it is fun and easy to read. I bet this dad wishes he could say the same about his daughter.

I'm tempted to take my chair over and strike up a conversation. I'd like to offer them hope that intimacy is still possible with their daughter, who probably feels like a stranger at their side.

But I don't think it's a good idea to give my opinion when it's not sought. I learned this years ago when I was dumb enough to think the girl I was dating would appreciate unsolicited fashion advice, so I suggested dressing like Julia Roberts would highlight her best qualities. I was thinking *Notting Hill*, but as it turned out, she thought I meant *Pretty Woman*.

Apparently girls don't like to be compared to hookers.

So I won't go over to them today, even though their passive reaction tells me they probably feel there's nothing they can do about their daughter. I meet lots of parents who feel that way. Their child goes through puberty, and what used to work no longer does, so they figure their only choice is to hang on and ride the waves of adolescent emotion as best as they can.

"That's just how teenagers are" they say, "so let's do what we can to maintain the peace, even if it costs us some dignity."

I feel compassion for anyone who sees things that way. I

imagine living in the shadow of iPhone girl's resentment must feel like living in Tornado Alley in early summer; just waiting and hoping the next storm doesn't bring too much damage.

*   *   *

It's difficult to look at a screaming spoiled brat with an ugly sense of entitlement and see anything more than selfishness. But as you know, there's something deeper going on than her apparent hatred of cheeseburgers.

While I feel for her parents, I also feel compassion for her. Even though I've never spoken to her, and although her behavior is inexcusable, I can see that she has a significant reason to resent her mom and dad.

When she tested them, their passivity stood as proof of one of the things she fears most: that she is more powerful than they are.

She made it clear she didn't want food, but what, exactly, *does* she want? If her childhood needs require something more from the adults in her life, then what should they be doing?

*   *   *

The best way I know to answer that is to tell you about something that happened years ago. It provides a perfect picture of what's going on inside young people when they test us. I remember it every time I'm tested at home, or in front of a crowd of teenagers, because it shows me what I need to do.

*   *   *

When I was living in Kauai, my realtor called and she said, "It just came on the market, and is exactly what you've been waiting for. It's an old pig farm, but don't let that scare you because it's a nice piece of land with a plantation cottage, and the price is right."

"I'm not scared; I like bacon."

"Great, meet you there at two."

I hung up and called my best friend Bruce on the mainland because I wanted to get his input on what to look for. He's a contractor, so he's much cooler than I am. He makes stuff with his hands that he can drive by later and tell his wife, "I built that."

All I ever get to say is, "I said words there."

Old ladies say words. So do some pretty birds.

I told him about the place and he said, "Okay, so before you fall in love with it, remember it's a plantation cottage, so it's different than most houses."

"In what way?"

"It has single-wall construction."

"What does that mean?"

"There's no bearing walls inside, and the outside walls are just tongue-and-groove planks that carry the entire weight of the roof and rafters."

"What's a bearing wall?"

Sigh.

"Just bring a rubber mallet, because you need to go around and bang on every board of the outside walls so you know how strong they are. If they're rotten or termite eaten, the house won't be safe."

"Um, okay."

"You don't own a rubber mallet do you?"

"I have a nice laptop and I man-scape."

"How is it possible I've never beaten you up?"

"Okay, so what do I do again?"

"Don't worry about the mallet; just go around and push and bang on all the outside walls, and keep track of how many boards are messed up. They don't have to be perfect; they just have to be strong. But put all your metrosexual weight into it, and don't fall in love with the place till you've done it."

I thanked him, and the second I saw the property I fell in love with it. It had me at Aloha. I wanted to tell the realtor to write the offer, but knew what I had to do first.

While I explained to her why I needed to push on the walls, I used a manly tone, as if it were my idea.

I took a deep breath and went around to every board and pushed, punched, kneed and kicked from top to bottom. She even found a ladder and held it for me so I could do the same on the outside. My heart was thumping, not only because of the height, but because I was afraid of what I'd discover since I already loved the place.

As I kept track, I grew happier because almost all the boards were solid and strong. When I was done, I turned, "It's safe. They're good. Let's make an offer."

We did, it was accepted, I moved in, and for years that little plantation cottage was a peaceful refuge.

And here's the point: *As I went around banging and pushing, I wasn't hoping that I was stronger than the walls, I was hoping they would be stronger than me.* That was the only way I could find assurance that the house would be safe enough to be my home.

When any child or teenager pushes against us, they are

hoping for the same thing. *They're not testing because they want us to give in. They're testing because their deeper need is to find reassurance we won't.*

*   *   *

As I write, I'm still sitting here on the sand, my stomach is still growling, and iPhone girl is taking selfies and posting them on Instagram. I was reluctant to sign up for Instagram at first. The name confused me. I thought it was a place to buy cocaine quickly.

But now I wonder, as she sits here posing for her phone, if she's at all like the many students who've confided in me. I suspect she is, which means she hasn't always felt such resentment. When her need to test arrived with puberty, it wasn't from the place of anger or bitterness it is today, but from the need to find safety in the midst of vulnerability. But then, as she continually discovered weakness where she needed strength, her pushing became more personal, more desperate, more angry.

When I began listening closely to the teenagers who were confessing their stories, I noticed a pattern. Their three top problems were family, then romance, then friendships, in that order, and those who felt most disgusted with their parents talked a lot about how their mom or dad weren't willing to stand behind the things they said were important.

Teenagers resent weakness.

I'm not suggesting that if iPhone girl's parents had stood up to her today, she would have hugged them and thanked them for being strong and said she'd take extra cheese on that burger. No, her resentment already runs so deep there's something else they need to do first, which we will get to later.

But I am saying that *all teenagers long for the adults in their lives to stand behind the things we say are important with consistent strength. And when we do, they will respect us, even when they disagree with our standards.*

This is as true in every classroom and living room as it is on this beach.

*   *   *

Our vacation ends this evening, so I'm about to pack up my beach chair for the last time. I just checked the weather back home and it's raining and cold, which means tomorrow I'll be writing to you while sitting by a fire in our little house in Laguna Beach, California.

From my chair near the fireplace there, I can see a painting of my old plantation cottage in Kauai, hanging on our wall. When we moved in, my wife Kristen hung it next to our front door. We look at it sometimes together and it reminds us what we need to do when one of our kids is a pain in the butt. It also helps us remember that their testing isn't really as personal as it feels, and that if we remain strong, it never will be.

I don't know if she hung it by the door for a special reason, but on at least one occasion, seeing it there stopped me from running out to bring back a priest for an exorcism.

The painting is important to me because I still feel deep affection for that little cottage. Its walls weren't perfect, but they stood firm against quite a few storms. I'm grateful I got to spend some important years living within the safety they provided.

I hope my children, and the students I work with, will look

back and feel the same about me.

There was a time before that cottage when I was convinced my children would rarely even speak to me. I'd done something so destructive I expected nothing but loneliness...

04

Hope
(A Personal Note)

I want to take a moment to let you know I'm not writing these pages from the lofty position of an expert – I'm no Dr. Phil – or from the perspective of a perfect family story. Every time I meet a "perfect family" I'm convinced they are in fact, some kind of front for a drug cartel.

On the contrary, my own story is one of brokenness. At its fulcrum is a choice I made when my sons were small that ended my marriage and hurt those I loved most. It brought the kind of despair into my life that can only come from a complete loss of hope.

My faith was dead, and things unraveled to the point that I found myself relying on the kindness of Chinese grocers to keep me alive. The thing that kept me moving forward was the notion that to give up would be to hurt my sons still more. I was convinced I'd forfeited my chance to live inside a beautiful story, but gratefully, I was wrong.

Emily Dickinson said hope "is a thing with feathers that perches in the soul, and sings the tune without the words, and never stops at all." I can't pretend to understand everything she meant, but hope did pursue and find me, and that's the theme of the next chapter.

While I've been lucky to have learned a lot from speaking to millions of teenagers, I'm luckier still to have maintained an amazing relationship with my sons, who are now in their twenties; to have been given the gift of their mom's forgiveness and friendship; and now to find my days filled with the laughter of a woman named Kristen (whom I've tricked into marrying me) and her three young children.

Everyone close to me, of course, knows my story. They know there were years when something hidden from my past held power over me. In this way I was like Moema, but the difference is, I really was guilty. I know she'd encourage me to tell you my story, which is what I've done, as an aside, in chapter 5. Parts will make you smile and others will offer you hope, regardless of what you're up against.

You can skip it if you like; it won't hurt my feelings.

With warmth,

Tyler

05

An Aside

Spring had reached the cul-de-sac before I had, her lazy breath moving through leaves and over fresh-cut grass.

I was putting the car in park when his blond hair caught my eye as he burst from the front door and leaped down two steps from the landing. Startled birds scattered as he hit the lawn at a full sprint.

Seeing him come at me signaled my stomach to switch to butterfly mode, wings all fluttering inside. I pushed the door and rushed to step out of the car as he rounded the back and jumped into my arms, almost knocking me back into my seat.

My seven-year-old son, his chest against mine, nothing better. It'd been three weeks since my last visit, and smelling Paul's hair and absorbing his energy made the heaviness of missing him disappear. For five years I'd been making this three-thousand-mile journey as often as I could.

As his feet dangled in mid-air I squeezed and kissed and did all kinds of other things little boys pretend to hate.

He giggled, "Dad. Dad! Stop! Guess what? Dad! Stop!"

Before he could talk, the other half of my heart came through the front door, all smiles and waves.

"Spence!" I shouted, as I started toward him, throwing Paul over my shoulder. Spencer was nine, and seeing him caused the butterflies to kick it up a notch.

"Dad!" Paul said, his head halfway down my back. "I'm trying to show you something!"

I set him down and noticed his hands were cupped as if cradling something fragile. Just then Laurie came through the front door. "He's been pretty excited for you to get here."

Paul bounced along as I walked toward the house, talking faster than two teenage girls after a school dance.

"Dad! I caught two little green tree frogs and kept them alive so you could see them and set them free with me and I love them and you can hold one but you have to be careful not to squish it so do you wanna see them now, do you, huh, do you?"

The frog wrangler and I stepped onto the landing. I grabbed Spencer to my chest, while trying to show Paul how excited I was about his web-footed friends. As a former seven-year-old boy, I was aware this was a pretty big deal.

My own dad was great about listening to my adventures, though sometimes he'd just shake his head and walk away. Like the time I told him I got beat up in the bathroom by a kid named John because I said his name fit well into any room with urinals. Apparently he was a tad sensitive about his name. And, as I found out months later in that same bathroom, so was his big brother Richard.

Paul reached out and carefully handed me my frog. Then, with his chest puffed out, he showed me his. It was smaller than his pinky nail and I could see why he loved it.

He said, "Wanna set them free now?" I nodded, and as I stepped off the landing, turned to ask Spencer if he wanted to join us in this important conservationist endeavor.

As the words were leaving my mouth, something terrible happened. I knew this by the anguish of Paul's scream.

"NOOOOOO!!!!!!!!"

I froze. My right foot down on the first step. Tears already streamed from Paul's eyes.

"What happened?" The words flew out of my mouth with some dead butterflies.

His little body convulsed. "You" sob "killed" sob "my" sob "frog!"

"No I didn't. Look Buddy, it's still here in my hand."

"Not that one!" Big breath. More tears. He pointed at my right foot.

"You stepped on mine!"

All our eyes turned toward that foot, and I whispered, "Oh God, please don't let this be!" But my prayer had come too late. I slowly lifted my foot, and there it was. Irrefutable evidence. Frog carcass. Squished love. Round wet circle of green death.

We all looked at Paul who was still staring at his broken friend.

He screamed it again. "You. Killed. My. Frog!"

I reached for him but he pulled away and ran into the house, crying all the way up the stairs.

Silence flowed onto the landing. We all looked at each other and then back at the wet spot. I couldn't believe it. This moment was supposed to be happy. A sweet reunion. But I'd been there less than sixty seconds and I'd already crushed my boy's frog.

What are the odds? The precision of the leap. The timing of my step. The precise nanosecond and trajectory coming together to place that frog under the shadow of my descending foot.

I knew it was just a frog, but these times with my boys were so important to me, and Paul's words had crashed into my gut with the force of a judge's gavel. Guilty as charged. And there was nothing I could do to fix it.

Sometimes I wish I was Jesus.

I handed Paul's other frog to Spencer and he chuckled, "You killed his frog."

I looked at Laurie, motioned toward the door, and she said, "Go ahead."

As I ran up the stairs I heard Spencer call behind me. "Hey Dad, want me to kill this one too?"

Brother.

When I reached the top of the stairs, I heard Paul crying in his room. I looked in but couldn't see him, then heard he'd taken refuge in the 10-inch space under his bed.

It hit me this was the first time something he loved had died. It also struck me there are millions of children his age experiencing true tragedy, and real loss. But pain is relative, and first pains are deep pains, so I knew I needed to be careful not to diminish the validity of what he was feeling. It was real to him, so it needed to be real to me.

When I bent to look at him, I saw he was facing the other way with his knees drawn up to his chest, so I went around to the other side and got down on the floor. As I did, he turned his back.

"Go away!"

Ouch!

I paused.

I didn't know what to do.

I'm aware sometimes, "Go away" means "Do you love me enough to persevere?" But I didn't know which kind this was.

I'm also aware sometimes "Go away" means, "Hey creepy old guy, you're sitting way too close to me in this coffee shop." But that's a different book.

So I just knelt there.

And that's when it began...

My emotions started to swirl, as old and long-suppressed hurts rose to the brim of my chest. Paul crying under his bed had become some kind of emotional trigger for me, and what it produced hit me like a tsunami. I was being sucked into an eddy of feelings I had tried to suppress since my divorce six years earlier.

I strained to pull myself free, but the rush of emotions was too strong. They were coming one after the other, like corpses that had unearthed themselves, each one carrying armfuls of shame.

I was kneeling there, but was simultaneously transported in my mind back in time to the edge of the Golden Gate Bridge, where I'd gone several times during the weeks following Laurie's remarriage and move. And now the wind was swirling around me again, and so was the self-loathing.

I'd been terrified my boys would grow up to think of me as a stranger. Or worse, to hate me for what I'd done. What else could they feel but disgust once they learned I'd had an affair when they were small, that my selfishness had crushed their mother's heart, and I'd betrayed the trust of everyone I cared for? I'd been led to that bridge by the feral imagining my sons might be better off without me.

That I might be better off without me.

Lost perspective is a cold wet fog, and shame is a cancer.

I'd been a young associate pastor in a large church, and our future had been bright. But then I confessed to Laurie, and her heart, along with our lives, was shattered. She took the boys and moved in with her mom, where she had long days followed by broken sleep that catapulted her between heartbreak and numbness.

It's been more than twenty-two years since I told her what I'd done, and I can still remember the ache in her voice when she asked how she could ever trust me again.

I had no answer.

When I confessed my affair to the head pastor, he wanted to find a way to restore me. But he didn't know, and I didn't explain, that the crisis of faith that led up to my choice, and the weeks of living a double life since, had been too much for me. I had nothing left.

And so my career was over, my severance pay signed willingly over to Laurie, my reputation and the only future I was trained for destroyed, and my faith long dead. I had hurt lots of people. Most vilified me and withdrew, and I understood why. But worse, my family was gone.

The silence that filled the last prepaid weeks in our apartment was weighted and pressed down on me. There were no sounds of boys playing down the hall, and each night I'd hear "Goodnight Daddy, I love you" over telephone lines, instead of through their bedroom door. When I reached to turn the lights off on another empty day, I'd see their faces in their photos instead of on their pillows.

I had done this to all of us, and it could not be undone.

If Emily Dickinson is right, and hope is a thing with feathers, I'd managed to reach in to where it was perched and crush its hollow bones.

*　　*　　*

The day I moved the few things I had left into storage, a widow named Donna, whose son I had helped a year earlier, saw me in a McDonald's. I'd never met her before, but she came over because she could see I was undone. Her own loss made it possible for her to recognize it in others.

She invited me to stay in the guest room in her basement, where I lived and rarely got out of bed for the next five months, except to visit my boys. Depression had become my tangible enemy, and she never judged me. She just showed kindness, until it became clear I wouldn't heal unless she asked me to leave. As she sat on the edge of the bed and told me why I had to go, her tears were proof she was doing it in love.

Her wisdom still stands as one of the greatest gifts poured out on my life.

In order to move forward, I buried my shame and tried to start my life over in a new place. I drove to San Francisco, where I found part-time work as a security guard and a cheap hotel to live in. It was the kind of place you can rent by the hour.

I hardly slept during the three months I lived there. There was one shared bathroom and shower on each floor. They were filthy, but it was all I could afford.

My education meant nothing in this new world, and I was ashamed of my weakness. I had no ambition or hope, so when the job ended because of the slow holiday season, I was forced to live in my car.

I'd park somewhere at night until the cops tapped on the window to tell me to move. Then I'd drive to a different corner or park under a different overpass. I was too embarrassed to ask my family for help, so this became my routine for the next six months.

I walked the streets at night feeling like a zombie. Everything was numb. My eyes were portals through which I viewed movement around me, and I felt separate from everything. Detached. Like I was watching an uncompelling movie about someone else's life from the inside. Though I could touch things, they felt distant, and the noises of the city were drowned out by the silence of the god I had always believed in.

It was a hollow kind of aching.

When I couldn't find odd jobs, I'd beg the small Chinese grocers for food. I'd stand there at their registers crying real tears until they'd give me an apple or banana if I promised to never come back.

The weeks dissolved into each other, and the only thing I had to cling to was the sound of my boys voices on the next scheduled phone call. They were living with another man by this time, a better man, and each night when I pulled the blanket over me in my passenger seat, I'd picture him tucking them in and kneeling to say nighttime prayers. He had bought them their first puppies, was their soccer coach and would teach them to ride their first two-wheeler, and I was just a trembling loss.

A leftover gym membership gave me a place to bathe, and I eventually found a job as a waiter, which helped me rent an apartment.

One day someone who'd heard me speak years earlier

approached me about speaking at a school. They didn't know what had happened in my life, and I didn't tell. I just said no for months. But they persisted, so I eventually accepted.

My shame kept me from real vulnerability that day, and the great irony was as a result of my secret pain, there was something in my speaking others could connect with. They told me I understood them, and so word of mouth gave birth to a speaking career. My clients were unaware of my personal story, and I never used it as a part of my material.

A booking agent suggested I change my first name. He told me my given name of Frank might look good on a truck driver's pocket or the back of a bowling shirt, but it didn't work well on a brochure. So I chose Tyler, leaving my last name intact. It became a reminder I had begun a new life.

And yet, as I discovered, a new name and address does little to chase away demons.

*   *   *

But now, here I was, six years later on Paul's floor, and the inevitable was happening. My unattended wounds were bursting.

A sob from beneath the bed pulled me back into the moment. The present, which had receded, came rushing back and I was hit by the fact I was kneeling there in my child's room, next to a bed and on a carpet provided by someone else.

A familiar heaviness settled into my gut.

Another sob. This time from my chest.

I knew I had to hold it together for Paul's sake, so I wiped my eyes, and yet I still didn't know what to do. He had said, "Go away."

Was he right? Should I? Did I even belong here?

But then something compelled me, like a whisper from God, and I knew what I needed to do.

I compressed my body into that ten-inch space, and moved in toward him. I had failed in the past, but this was my son, and I needed to go and be where he was.

I slid up behind him as I worked the bed over me, and attempted to spoon him. As I reached, he shrugged my arm off and scooted a little further away.

Then he said it again.

"Go away!"

The lump caught in my throat.

But I stayed.

He needed me to.

I needed me to.

A moment passed, and although he was still crying and the space between us was full of questions, I breathed out a whisper.

"Paul, I'm sorry I killed your frog."

And I was sorry for so much more.

The air was still, nothing moved, and then a wonderful thing happened.

He leaned his back into my chest.

I wrapped my arm around him, and said it again.

Paul, I'm so sorry."

"It's" sob "okay Dad" sob "I know you didn't mean to."

His forgiveness washed over me. I received it, and discovered it had brought something else with it. Something with feathers.

And I knew, for the first time in all the years, I now needed to forgive myself. Not for the frog, but for all the other things I could never change. I didn't know it yet, but that singular understanding was the beginning of the greatest healing in my life.

As I lay there, I felt hope warm me. It was seeping through his back into my chest.

*   *   *

We stayed still for a little while, and then talked about other important stuff, like death, and how we need each other.

I told him I was learning that when we're sad, we shouldn't try to handle it alone. That it's good to talk about things.

I said it more for myself than him.

"I already know that Dad."

"You're pretty smart then, Buddy."

We were both quiet again, and it felt comfortable.

We decided it would be good to crawl out, find an empty matchbox, and go have a funeral. We placed the deceased in its coffin, and Paul disappeared into the house. He came back holding popsicles, so we could use the sticks to make a cross. We put the funeral on hold, sat in the sun with Spencer and we all enjoyed our frozen juice on a stick.

Healing was happening.

While we ate, Spencer suggested we do the kind thing and crush the other frog too, in order to help it avoid the lonely life it was destined to lead without its dead friend.

My son, Spencer Kevorkian. Mr. Euthanasia. The Doctor of Death. I thought how his sweet gift of empathy would be helpful in life.

We fixed the sticks together and Paul wrote "Dead Frog" on the cross-member with a Sharpie. The funeral was respectful.

Laurie attended, and we all said something nice.

We set the other frog free in the woods and got in the car to head off for our weekend together. As we drove away, I heard Paul in the backseat say, "What kind of a dad shows up and smushes his little kid's frog?"

The boy has a hard heart.

*　　*　　*

When I drove away after our weekend, I was smiling. Not only because Paul had forgiven me for the frog, but because I could still feel the flutter of wings in my soul.

A few years later, when Laurie and I agreed they were old enough, I told them about my greatest failures. They forgave me then, as they still do now.

They've taught me forgiveness is more powerful than shame, and it carries redemption in its arms.

And as far as I can tell, Spencer still hasn't assisted in any suicides, frog or otherwise. This makes me happy, especially since he's the chief editor of this book, and I don't want legal trouble.

06

They Need to Hear the Words

When I was nine I had a crush on a nun. Her name was Maria.

I saw her in *The Sound of Music* and told my older brother I was going to marry her. He told me I was dumb because she was dating Jesus, which didn't seem fair to me.

I drifted to sleep that night singing, "How do you solve a problem like Maria? How do you steal her from the Son of God?"

When I woke I wondered if she'd be impressed with how long I could do a wheelie on my banana-seat Schwinn. But then I heard Jesus had raised an actual dead guy from the grave, so I knew I was screwed.

My brother told me later all the nuns were dating Jesus, and this really messed with my head. It had a profound effect on my early ideas of God.

And of nuns.

But then I grew up and sorted out all the confusion. Over time I had the chance to meet some actual nuns, and several of them became my friends.

*   *   *

My favorite of these is Sister Catherine. She called and asked if I'd come speak at the all-girls high school she runs. I'd been there before, and she wanted to know if I'd come back and focus on the subjects of "dating, romance and sex."

As she asked, I interrupted and said, "I'm sorry Sister, but my cell just dropped out for a second. You said 'dating, romance and what?'"

"And sex."

I sighed, "You'll never believe it but someone just sneezed. Can you repeat that?"

"Sex." She said a bit louder.

"Sex?"

"SEX!"

Then a giggle danced across the line and I knew she'd figured out I was just trying to see how many times I could get a nun to say the word sex.

"I know what you're doing Tyler, and I'm not going to say it again."

"Four times makes me very happy Sister; thank you."

"You're a bad man."

"I know I am."

We laughed and went on to plan the day.

Sister Catherine is five feet tall and embodies the full joy of God's love.

The day arrived and I stood to speak about those topics to over a thousand girls, while thirty nuns stared at me from the back wall where they sat in a row decked out in their habits and beads.

It felt like God was watching me.

I'd promised the girls that at the end of the day I'd answer any questions they had. I told them no question was off limits, there was a box they could use anonymously, and I'd randomly pull their questions and do my best with them.

I finished my final keynote and asked for the box. As I reached inside I said, "And here's the first one."

Because I wanted to honor my promise to answer any question, I read it aloud without first reading it to myself.

This plan was flawed.

"How come boys like big boobs better than small boobs?"

The girls giggled and I tried not to look at anyone in particular.

I became acutely aware that I was the only male in the room, and at the exact same moment every nun across the back leaned forward in her chair and tilted her head just slightly to the side.

Their motion was so precise and synchronized it seemed like they'd practiced it together in nun school. They were the Religious Rockettes.

I took a breath and it felt like God had just shushed all the angels and leaned over the balcony of Heaven to see what I'd say.

I fumbled mentally because I was trying to remember how Maria was built in that movie, thinking this might be a good place to start.

My brain isn't always efficient under pressure.

I looked at Sister Catherine in the back row. She smiled and nodded, and I knew I needed to tell the truth.

"Well, I can't speak for all boys, but I've dated women with different kinds of bodies, and all I can tell you is that the sexiest person I've ever dated had very small..."

And my brain froze. Inside my head, nothing but empty

space. I tried to find a word, any word, but I was paralyzed.

While everyone waited, the words I'd just said swung over the crowd like a church bell, resounding again and again "the sexiest person I've ever dated had very small..." "the sexiest person I've ever dated had very small..." – and so on.

In my muddled brain I realized I'd just said "sexiest" as though there was some sexy scale in my mind or something, which there is, but this went against all the ideals I'd spoken about all day.

I knew I had to complete my sentence and wondered if it was okay to say "boobs" since it was in the question. I decided to go with the anatomical word, but couldn't find it in my brain anywhere. I could think of lots of other words used around town for this body part, but the word "breasts" eluded me.

I gulped. It jumped into my mind. So I blurted it out with more fervor than I should have.

"Breasts!"

And then – silence.

Everyone sat there looking at me.

All of this made me miss Maria. She would've known what to say, or sing. I love how she'd break into spontaneous song at just the right moment, but the only song that came to my mind was, "These are a few of my favorite things," which seemed inappropriate, given the question at hand.

Later, on the airplane I would think of all the great answers I should have given. The ones that have to do with a woman's real value and that her visual appeal has more to do with how she carries and feels about herself than her shape, and that true beauty comes from the inside, and how temporary physical beauty is anyway, and all that.

But as I stood there I had nothing.

I shook my head just a bit and said my next words quickly to try and distract everyone from the boob debacle.

"So-I'm-not-sure-it's-true-that-all-boys-feel-that-way-about-the-size-of-um-well-you-know-um-so-let's-look-at-another-question-shall-we?" And I reached back into the box. To my relief the rest of the answers came easily.

The box was so full I couldn't get to all the questions, which helps me understand why I meet so many girls across North America who've made life-changing mistakes with boys. Too many questions and not enough safe places to ask.

After the Q&A, everyone applauded and I was happy I'd soon be out of the sea of estrogen. I was afraid that Sister Catherine was going to be mad at me, so I headed for the opposite side of the room. My plan was to stay long enough to be polite, then make my escape.

I chatted for a few minutes with some of the students and nuns, and just as I was about to leave, a twelfth-grade girl named Keiko came over and asked if she could get some advice.

I said I'd help if I could, and we found a couple of folding chairs.

She explained she'd been dating a boy for five months, and her parents just told her they only wanted her seeing boys who were both Japanese and Roman Catholic, of which he was neither.

I asked how she'd responded, and she said she'd told them she'd honor their wishes, and asked if they'd be willing to get to know him and his family better when she turned eighteen. They'd agreed.

"Do you think I'm handling this the right way?"

I smiled and told her I thought she was, saying she'd not only respected her boyfriend and parents, but she'd also respected herself.

"You really think so?"

"Absolutely. In fact you ought to write a book for girls. The way you're handling this thing shows tons of wisdom."

She thanked me, even though I'd done little, and stood to go. As she did I said, "I'm proud of you, Keiko."

When the words crossed the space between us, she collapsed back into her metal chair with such force that everyone in the room looked our way. It was as if the muscles in her legs had failed. As she landed, she burst into tears.

I froze in my seat. I had no idea what had just happened.

Everyone in the room had stopped talking. I was afraid Sister Catherine was going to come over and hit me with a Bible or something.

Keiko's tears were gushing.

All I could figure was she must have misunderstood what I'd said; so I said it again, only this time slower and louder.

"I'm proud of you."

This seemed to make her cry harder, which confused me.

Sometimes males don't understand females. I know this because I have a wife.

I sat there feeling helpless and decided to keep my mouth shut, which I've learned is the best strategy when in the presence of a crying female.

As I waited, she calmed herself and said, "I'm sorry."

She was wiping her face and I was still afraid of saying something stupid. I'd spent a lot of money on my master's degree, but again had nothing relevant in my head.

I should have studied harder.

She took a deep breath and settled her shoulders, "It's just that my mom and dad have never said they're proud of me. Not even once."

She said it quietly, as if telling herself a secret.

Her tears swelled again.

"Never?"

"Never."

Some of us spend our life healing from the hurts of our childhood. I know a successful fifty-something New York book publicist who read about Keiko and it brought him to tears. He said his whole life he's longed to hear those words from his dad.

I leaned toward her, "I'm sorry Keiko."

"Nothing I ever do is good enough for them." Her eyes were full of longing.

There are those who think the best way to love a child is to push them to try harder and do better, without ever taking time to praise them for their inner beauty. These people don't know this bears one of two results. They may get a child who believes nothing they do is good enough, so they stop trying – or one who connects outward success to their inner worth, and measures their value solely on their performance.

Either is a miserable way to live.

Perhaps this is why at a recent student leadership conference with 1800 students, 82% of them confessed to me on an anonymous 3 X 5 card that their greatest emotion as they looked to the future wasn't excitement or eagerness, but the fear of failure.

I smiled at Keiko and said, "Well I'm proud of you, and if

my daughter Brooke grows up to be anything like you, I'd be grateful."

She could tell I meant this, blinked new tears and said, "Thank you. I'll never forget you said that."

I think it's hard to be a girl these days, and the rest of us can make their journey easier.

We talked for a few more minutes then as she walked away a lot of emotions were left floating in her wake. I don't know how long I stood there, but a touch on my arm jerked me from my thoughts.

It was Sister Catherine. She'd snuck up and put her hand on my elbow. I think her habit was some kind of cloak of silence or something.

I looked down at her, and my heart stopped because I'd never been yelled at by a nun before. Weird, but right then I wondered what someone could possibly give a nun for her birthday.

Sneakers? Do they ever jog or play tennis? Do nuns even have feet?

She raised her pointer finger and signaled me to lean down. I inhaled and bent to listen.

"Tyler."

It was just a whisper.

"Yes."

"You handled that boob question quite well." She patted my arm and smiled.

Phew! It was nice to know God wasn't mad at me.

"And I heard what you just said to Keiko, and I want you to know *I'm* proud of you!"

I didn't know if it was okay to hug a nun or not, but I gave her a big one anyway, my face pressed against the side of her vale and cheek. She smelled clean.

She hugged me back and as she did, I realized that perhaps I had needed to hear those words as much as Keiko.

I suppose we all do.

After the hug Sister Catherine grabbed both my hands and said, "If I had a son, and I'm pretty sure I never will, I'd want him to be just like you." And her words caught in my throat.

I nodded a moist-eyed thank you.

*   *   *

When I got to my rental car another girl stepped in front of me. I never caught her name because she only stayed long enough to ask a question, and left before she could hear an answer.

She was holding a teenage magazine just below her chin. There on the cover was the typical airbrushed model smiling out at me, and just above it, sadness in her own eyes.

Her question. Why can't this be me?

I started to speak but she held up her hand and quieted me. She shook her head, turned to leave, and stuffed the magazine into her backpack, her pain back into her heart, and ran to mix in with all the other girls crowding onto the bus.

Sometimes I think we ask questions not so much to find answers, but as a way to feel less alone.

As I sat in traffic on the way to the airport, I couldn't chase her words or expression from my mind. I looked at my watch and realized my own ten-year-old Brookie was riding her school bus to our house at that same moment. It made me wonder if she knows that her value isn't based on the shape of her cheekbone, or the angle of her jaw.

I barely made my flight and as I boarded the plane, it occurred to me I get so absorbed with helping Brookie learn stuff, I forget to say the reasons I cherish her.

*   *   *

Late that night, as Kristen and I pulled the covers up over the end of the day, I told her all about my trip, and confessed I'd developed a little crush on Sister Catherine. She said it was okay, since Maria never calls.

*   *   *

Sister Catherine, I know you're reading this somewhere, and I just want to say I think Keiko and the girl with the magazine are blessed to be attending your school.

I also want you to know I think Jesus is pretty lucky to be dating you.

07

They Need to *Earn* the Words

Matthew transferred into my tenth-grade lit class a few days into my first week as a teacher. I liked him at first, but soon noticed things that rubbed me the wrong way. It turned out he was having the same effect on my colleagues, and we attributed it to the hints of arrogance we could sense in the ways he moved and talked.

You could catch him staring at his reflection in the windows, or notice how he slouched back and sighed if his hand was up and someone else was chosen, or pick up on the condescending tone in his answers when called on.

Though it would've been tough to prove exactly why, any interaction left the unmistakable impression he thought he was cooler, more important and smarter than you.

His peers kept him at arms distance, so he hovered around the periphery of their circles without seeming to notice he was never invited in. His pride in the extravagant lunches his mom packed for him seemed to distract him from the fact he often ate alone.

He was intelligent but always did just enough to get by, and the thing that bothered me most was he never took responsibility for anything. If I'd tell him to stop talking in class, he'd say, "Eric asked me a question" or "Sofia was talking too!" His excuses had an air of sincerity because his self-love made him blind to his faults. At most he believed he was misheard, misquoted or misunderstood, but never wrong.

I remember wishing I could help him see how ugly these traits were, until a phone call convinced me doing so might be impossible.

*   *   *

It was about 7:30 pm and I had low blood sugar. I was standing in the kitchen watching some leftover lasagna spin in the microwave when the phone rang. I should've let it go to voicemail, but I get a little dumb when I'm hungry.

I tried to sound perky. "This is Tyler."

"Hi Mr. Durman. My son's in your class. Do you have a minute to talk?"

I was a new teacher, so I assumed it was a parent calling to thank me. Something like, "We're all sitting around talking about important people and your name came up, so we've written a poem and set it to music and you're on speaker so we can sing it and you should expect a gift in the mail this week."

Naiveté can be soothing.

I thought I could serve her better if we talked after I'd eaten, so I said, "Well actually, I'm just putting my dinner on the table, so maybe I could call back in..."

She didn't let me finish, "I've got a busy evening so I'd like to talk now."

"Um, okay."

"We just got his progress report and think there must be a mistake."

"What's your son's name?"

"Matthew."

"Ah, Matthew. Doesn't like being called Matt does he?"

Not even a pause. "That's because we named him Matthew, not Matt."

I could tell she hadn't spent the last hour with a good masseuse.

"It seems you've given him a C, and I'm wondering what we can do about that?"

"We? Well there's nothing *we* can do, but I'd be happy to work with him. This is just a progress report so..."

"I understand, but our older twins always get A's and we're afraid this will make him feel defeated."

"While I appreciate your..."

"My husband and I know you're a new teacher..."

She deserved an A in interrupting.

I sat down as she continued, "and I'm sure you know grades reflect as much on the teacher as the student, so I wouldn't think you'd want such a popular boy feeling bad about your class."

Did I mention I had low blood sugar?

"While I appreciate your concern, I'm sorry but I can't change his grade. But as I said I'm willing..."

And with this, she upped her grade to an A+ for extra credit.

"We think if you'd change it, he'd feel better and work harder. Self-esteem has always been important to us, so I'm sure you'll understand why I'm pressing you on this."

"Yes, but I can't just give him a grade he didn't earn."

"If you'd be willing to meet, maybe we could find some middle ground."

Deep breath.

"I'd be happy to meet, but you need to know I'm not going to change his grade. But as I said..."

"I get the feeling you don't like my son."

And I shouldn't have said it. But I was young and hungry, and my lasagna was getting cold.

"Well the truth is, I don't."

It was wrong, but it felt soooo good!

Angry now, "I can't believe you said that! Everyone loves our Matthew. What kind of a teacher would say that?"

I was a young fool, and on a roll.

"The kind of teacher who'd probably like your son a lot more if he didn't have a mother who'd call to cover for the consequences of *his* behavior!"

In my mind I was in a Southern church and the congregation was shouting, "Preach it Tyler! Preach it!"

She didn't even offer an "Amen!"

Yelling now, "I can't believe this! I'm calling the principal!"

I made my voice raspy, like Clint Eastwood's.

"Fine! Want his number?"

"Already have it!"

"Figured you would!"

She hung up and I thought "Oh Crap!"

As I climbed into bed I felt more like Shirley Temple than Clint Eastwood, and spent most the night tossing and preparing my defense for the principal's office in the morning. I'd been there a lot as a student, so I knew how little time there'd be for explanations.

I arrived early and asked his secretary if he was in.

"You'd better get in there. He told me to get you as soon as you were on campus."

Yikes!

Mr. LaCross was a small but powerful man. When I poked my head in, he said, "Sit!" without looking up from his paperwork.

I should have brought donuts.

After a long minute he stood and came around in front of me. I started to say something and he said, "Keep your mouth shut."

This made it clear donuts wouldn't have helped.

"Two things."

His tone was stern.

"First, if you ever talk to a parent that way again, I will not only fire you, I'll make it my mission to see you never get another teaching job anywhere on the planet. Do you understand?"

I nodded and glanced at the floor as a sign of contrition.

"Second," his voice softened, "thank you for saying that to that woman, I've been dying to say it myself since her twins were freshman."

I smiled.

"Don't smile. Get out!" He pointed to the door and headed around his desk. I was gone before he reached his chair.

As I passed his secretary she said, "That's why I love working for him."

Another nod, and I walked out having learned a new reason it's hard to be a teacher, you have to keep your mouth shut even when parents are condescending and insulting. I think it would be more fun if teachers and parents could just climb into cage-fighting rings and duke it out. It'd raise a lot of money for the PTA.

*   *   *

Looking back on that phone call with the benefit of years and a family of my own, I've also learned how hard it is to be a parent.

In fact, it sucks sometimes!

I know that's not a very classy sentence, but it's the raw truth and I think we should give ourselves permission to say it to someone when we feel it.

While being a dad is the single most meaningful experience of my life, it can also be exhausting and overwhelming. The fact that we love our kids means they have the ability to hurt us in ways no one else can.

On top of that, sometimes they're just plain annoying. Last night I asked our easiest child Caleb to take the dogs for a walk and he reacted like I'd asked for a kidney. I said we'd talk about his attitude when he got back, and as he left with the dogs I frankly enjoyed the idea he'd be picking up poop while he was gone.

Time magazine did an article with research proving it's a myth having children makes people happier. I showed it to the kids at dinner and said they'd better get rich one day to pay us back for all the vegetables they've complained about eating.

Their laughter reminded me why my life might be an exception to *Time's* research.

*   *   *

It hasn't always been this way in our culture.

Being a parent or teacher is hard, but both have been made more difficult by some things a lot of "parenting experts" began preaching in the 1960s.

These experts found their voice during the cultural upheaval of that decade and began talking a lot about self-esteem. This was helpful until, in the decades that followed, they took things too far and turned the American family on its head.

Home was traditionally an adult-centered place in our country, which was best for kids because it taught them they were not the center of the world, but then new "experts" said things that seemed intuitively correct, and unfortunately convinced parents that home should be child-centered places.

I suspect Matthew's mom was listening to their advice, which is why she was blindly raising a narcissist. Here's how such a radical transition happened while we weren't looking....

Mike and Millie were expecting twins.
They had lots of questions but didn't know where to turn.

They decided to listen to some smart guys with PHD's
who said, "Self-esteem is important!"
This was a good thing.

So as the twins grew, Mike and Millie affirmed them **after** they did things to **earn** a good self-esteem.

But then the experts started saying they should **instill** a good self-esteem, so Mike and Millie started affirming the twins and their new little brother Matthew even when they hadn't done anything good. So the kids no longer had to earn a good self-esteem because they were getting it for **free**.

As time went by, the experts took it even further and said they should **protect** their kids from anything or anyone who could make the kids feel bad. This felt right to Mike and Millie's intuition, so their home became a **child-centered place**.

This taught the twins and Matthew anything that makes you feel bad should be avoided. They started thinking it was their parent's job to keep them happy, so they got lazy and never took responsibility.

Mike and Millie loved their kids and were working very hard to keep them **protected** and **happy**. All this made them tired and lonely.

They believed the best way to love their kids was to serve them all the time, and they didn't know what to do when the kids were disrespectful, demanding and ungrateful. They figured that's just how teenagers are, so they served them harder and even did their homework. This left no time for their marriage and they were growing apart.

The experts got their own TV shows, and nothing Mike and Millie did was good enough for the kids, who started resenting them. Matthew was only nice when he wanted something, and home was a pretty unhappy place

They'd worked really hard to be loving parents,
but after the kids moved out, Mike and Millie
didn't know each other anymore, and their kids
never called, except when they needed money.

Matthew became such a lazy **narcissist** his wife kicked him out and he moved back in with Mike and Millie when he was 32. He said he was going to write a self-help book but never got off the couch or put down the remote control.

Parents with child-centered homes are sincere, but are also more likely to act like peers than parents. They tend to struggle balancing their desire to feel close to their kids, with discipline.

* * *

Counterintuitive

On the surface it seems logical that if we love our kids, we should serve and protect them in every way we can. But as Matthew and others like him prove, child-centered homes are not good for anyone.

We don't serve our kids well by being their servants.

Yet there are dozens of books available today that encourage child-centered homes. The ideas in their pages feel good because they appeal to our intuition, but in the end they are destructive.

One writer suggests if your daughter says, "I'm bored," you should interrupt what you're doing to help her figure out what to do. This, it says, will teach her to make choices on her own. The problem is this reinforces her expectation that life should be a string of uninterrupted pleasures, and when it's not, that it's the responsibility of adults around her to fix the problem of her unhappiness.

It makes me think of Matthew huffing when his hand was up and someone else was chosen. He was sincerely offended because the adult in the room hadn't catered to his wants. He viewed the world like a movie in which he was playing the lead, and everyone else played supporting roles.

There's no addiction so powerful as self-addiction.

When I was growing up and said I was bored, my mom never said, "Well let me bring my life to a screeching halt so you can be entertained." Nope, she said, "If you're bored it's because you're boring, so get out from under my feet and find something to do, or I'll give you a chore!"

Her generation was far from perfect, yet it strikes me that despite how harsh those words may seem, I never once doubted her love or sulked away nursing a damaged self-esteem. I just went outside and played.

My parents believed their role in my life was to prepare me for the realities of the world outside our home and not to focus on how I was or wasn't feeling at a given moment. Happiness was never the ultimate goal; loving others was.

Chores weren't done for money. They were there to provide an opportunity to contribute to the needs of the family. We knew the family didn't exist to keep us happy; we existed for the wellbeing of the family. This was another way of teaching us that the needs of others were more important than our own wants, and that our lives would take on added meaning if we lived for something outside ourselves.

There's a book today that says you shouldn't tell your son, "Go clean your room." Instead, it says, you should give him the choice to clean it now or later. The idea is that making him do it immediately diminishes his sense of self-worth, because it takes away his power to choose for himself.

The problem is this bears no resemblance to real life. I've never been pulled over by an officer who said, "Would you like to obey the speed limit now, or do you want to obey it later?" And the IRS never wrote saying, "This year or next; you choose."

A veteran principal whose high school was selected as a California Distinguished School last year told me she's lost most of the time she used to spend mentoring teachers, because of the hours taken by disgruntled parents. And a middle school principal in Oregon told me her most recent headache is parents who deliver fast food to their kids at lunch. It was causing chaos in the front office, and when she said it was no longer allowed, kids threw a fit and parents kept sneaking it to them over the fence.

It's no wonder that after visiting the United States, the Duke of Windsor said, "The thing that impresses me most about America is the way parents obey their children."

*   *   *

The Upside

I heard the story of a man who was shipwrecked on a remote island and built a hut for shade and to protect the few things he'd been able to salvage from the weather. He sat in it for hours each day staring out to sea hoping to see a boat he could signal, but months passed and none came. Late one afternoon he was searching for food when a sudden thunderstorm erupted. He rushed back to find his hut in flames, and everything he owned destroyed. He was despairing as he drifted into fitful sleep that night, but was startled awake by the voice of a stranger saying, "We saw your smoke signal and have come to rescue you."

I'm optimistic about our culture because all the bad smoke created by child-centered homes has caught the attention of some people who are doing pretty cool things in response.

In spite of the many Matthews, I'm now meeting unprecedented numbers of teenagers who've experienced the emptiness of living for self, and watched the damage done by selfish bullies in their schools and in the world, who are creating tangible organizations to bring social change. I wish I had time to tell you their stories. They would encourage you.

I was invited to a "Social Entrepreneurial Camp for Young Change-Makers" this summer that will feature teenage thought leaders as speakers, and will be attended by other teenagers who are hungry to learn how to apply business-like discipline and innovation to their causes.

I've also noticed the parent groups I speak to are radically different than they were ten years ago. It used to be like preaching to the choir, with only those who didn't need help showing up. But now the groups are larger, and for the first time include a majority of parents who are willing to be honest about their confusion, hurt, and hunger for answers. When I explain that good parenting is counterintuitive, and why child-centered homes aren't good for anyone, many of them wait when the meeting is over to seek advice because they're living with the negative results of their own child-centered homes. Their numbers and hunger make me believe we're primed for a cultural shift toward better parenting.

The media's focus on the "bullying epidemic" has created smoke that's being noticed in most communities. While I feel deeply for suffering families, I also believe the attention this issue is getting will help our culture realize that child-centered homes are feeding both sides of the problem. They not only produce more bullies, but in a peculiar twist, also produce children who are more likely to become victims.

These homes are creating teenagers like Matthew who see themselves as the star in their own movie, with everyone else as less important supporting actors. A 2010 University of Michigan study shows that college students today are 40 percent less empathetic than they were thirty years ago. This is startling! This means the average teenager's ability to connect with the feelings of others is being stunted, which makes them more likely to bully or be a silent bystander.

Child-centered homes also produce kids who are less likely to learn how to stick up for themselves or even believe they have the strength to do so, since their parents have always done it for them. This makes them more apt to come across weak and vulnerable when faced with conflict, which attracts bullies.

All this is causing us to seek answers that I believe will point us forward, toward caring adult-centered homes where parents recognize they build intimacy with their kids by being a parent first, and not a peer, and where kids see themselves as a grateful participant in society, and not the most valuable person in it.

We're growing weary of the Matthews and beginning to see that the best way to help teachers is to hand them kids who don't think of themselves as the star, and to support teachers when they discipline the students who do.

These are all significant reasons to hope.

*   *   *

Two things I learn from Matthew's mom.

1. It's important to ask the right questions.

His mom was focused on this, "Is my son happy, or do I need to protect him today?"

She would have served him better by asking, "Is my son living with generosity, humility and kindness, and is he behaving responsibly? If not, what privileges should he lose so he'll learn he's not more important than others and that the world won't cater to his feelings?"

Matthew's narcissism is proof that while all teenagers need to hear we're proud of them, they also need to know those words will mean more if they come *after they've earned them.*

2. Teachers are like vampires.

Vampires: When hunting these immortals, it's important to remember silver bullets are effective. But since silver bullets are hard to come by, you should only fire them in life-and-death situations. If you waste them, you'll be helpless when you need one most.

Teachers: They are not immortal; however, some of them are very pale from being inside all day. If we run to them for every little thing, we waste our silver bullets and they will stop listening, even when we need them to the most.

This is also true of administrators, coaches and spouses.

*　　*　　*

There's an ironic yet beautiful thread through all this. When we give ourselves permission to make teenagers unhappy sometimes, we put ourselves in the best position to have a close relationship with them.

Although when I first met "Alpha," I thought he was going to contradict this fact with his fist...

08

They Want to Respect Us More Than Like Us

When I walked into the gym, hundreds of students were crowding onto a single set of aging bleachers that were designed to hold a much smaller load. The tired wood sagged beneath the burden and seemed to groan along with the students as they climbed on its back.

He chose to sit front and center.

This was a continuation high school, which meant these kids had been unable to succeed in mainstream schools, and this was their last chance at a diploma. Like most other schools of this type, this one was underfunded and held together by a small group of educators who care deeply about kids.

His girlfriend sat behind him and he was leaning back between her legs with an arm slung over each of her thighs. The cotton of his white V-neck tee was stretched to its limit across his massive chest and shoulders. If the shirt's maker had sown in vocal cords, we would have heard it grunting as it strained at the seams.

He was an alpha male with a back as broad as a barn, so given their seating arrangement I figured his girlfriend's future was secure, since Cirque Du Soleil can always use an extra contortionist.

I was standing with the teachers on the side of the gym as the principal, a tall thin man, took the microphone to introduce me. When he spoke, everyone quieted, save two.

The sheer mass of Alpha's body had drawn my attention, but what kept it was the volume of his voice. He was ignoring social cues, I assumed on purpose, by talking over his shoulder and making his girlfriend laugh.

The principal was pretending not to notice, and I didn't judge him since he was saying nice things about me. Watching Alpha I thought he would've been perfectly cast to play the lead in *Fight Club*, and probably wouldn't morph into a giggling Winnie the Pooh once I took the microphone.

This meant things were about to get interesting.

Some of the teachers were clearly annoyed with Alpha's behavior, and one of them caught my eye with something like pity in her expression that said, "Hope you gave someone the name of your next-of-kin."

Of all the convictions I hold dear, two were pertinent to my current situation.

One: When my stomach's growling, as it was at that moment, there's nothing more magical than eating warm grilled cheese dipped into tomato soup, which I hoped to do soon at the Denny's I'd spotted down the street. If you've never had such an experience, you've never lived.

And two: When an adult is in front of a group of teenagers, all the students should face forward, sit quietly, and pay attention. And if they don't, the person up front should make sure they do. *It's our job to set the tone in our relationship with teenagers, because everything stands or falls on the question of respect.*

This second conviction meant I was probably going to have

to make a decision regarding Alpha that might preclude my ability to enjoy the first, since it's difficult to suck a sandwich through a straw.

Everything about him, including the way he sat sprawled out as if the bleachers were his throne and we his humble servants, screamed he wanted the world to know he was unmovable, in command, and the ultimate tough guy. I found myself wondering what wounded part of his story was at play in all the posturing.

I was lost in these thoughts when a smattering of applause and the sight of the principal holding the microphone in my direction startled me. I jogged to the center, and without preamble dove into my first story, saying...

"When I randomly picked him from the huge crowd, I was shocked because everyone jumped to their feet and started shouting his name. Within seconds they were stomping and chanting, 'Joe, Joe, Joe, Joe...' The air was throbbing!"

I had them.

Everyone that is, except Alpha.

Tough guys are usually insecure guys, so it didn't surprise me when it took less than a minute for him to test me. He tilted his head back and said something loud enough to draw attention to himself, but soft enough so I couldn't make out his words. As his girlfriend and others nearby laughed, he looked me up and down with a smirk that said, "What're you gonna do about it?"

Since I was a kid, a strange thing happens in my brain when I'm faced with conflict. It defaults to the question of what Clint Eastwood would say or do at that particular moment. I think I watched too many cowboy movies as a kid, and should probably walk around wearing a WWCD bracelet.

In my present circumstance I was pretty sure Clint would step closer to Alpha and say something like, "Hey punk, if you don't shut up and lean out of your girlfriend's cervix and treat me with respect, I'm gonna kick your good-for-nothing-juiced-up butt around this gym. Understand, Princess?"

Clint is cool.

I am not.

So because of Alpha's size, I decided a different tactic was needed.

* * *

Before we go on, I want to say something clearly, and not lightly. *The most important thing I've learned from teenagers is that the issue of Respect is the single most significant nonnegotiable if we want to influence their lives and have a close relationship with them. It's either the best building block we have for developing intimacy, or the biggest stumbling block. There is no middle ground.*

They want to respect us more than they want to like us – and if they don't respect us, they definitely won't like us.

If they discover we care too much about being liked, or that we aren't willing to take a stand on the small issues of Respect, they'll resent us for being weak, and see us as obstacles to be managed or manipulated until they're out from under our authority.

They're not done on the inside, so even after we've proven worthy of their Respect, they'll continue to test it because they need it in order to feel safe. Testing it is their subconscious way of asking, "Can I trust you to be there for me?"

* * *

All eyes shifted from Alpha back to me. His disrespect was so blatant everyone was going to make their own decisions about me based on how I responded.

I looked up to the crowd and said, "Excuse me, this'll only take a moment."

As I lowered the microphone, knowing full well everyone would be straining to hear what I'd say, things grew so still you could've heard a drop of sweat hit the gym floor. He was still smirking as I spoke to him, and I tried to keep my voice steady.

"I understand you might not want to be here, but don't talk anymore. It's okay if you don't listen, it really won't hurt my feelings, but the stuff we're going to talk about is important and might help someone here, so I'm not going to let anything get in the way of that. You can daydream if you want, but if you test me on this, I'll stop again and ask you to go stand over there with the teachers. Does this make sense to you?"

All eyes turned to him and he knew it.

He mumbled, "Whatever."

I said, "That's good enough. Thanks for listening." I raised the mic and jumped back into my story about Joe (which I can't wait to tell you in our next chapter.)

I used to make the mistake of trying to demand respect because of my position as an adult in authority. While I think teenagers should show respect to all adults by default, I've found it's not all that compelling to a kid who doesn't yet respect me.

Pulling rank can also come across like I'm reacting in weakness because my ego or feelings are hurt, which makes it feel personal. I've found it best to calmly explain that there are bigger reasons I expect what I do, and to do it with as few words as possible, so it doesn't feel like a lecture.

At home with our kids, the bigger reason Kristen and I give is that it's our job to prepare them to have success in the world outside our doors, and treating others with respect is central to that. In a classroom or assembly, the bigger reason I give is that what we're doing is important, and allowing anything to get in the way of it isn't good for others. The beautiful thing about these reasons is no one can argue with them, and they have nothing to do with feeling hurt or wanting to be liked.

It's rare I have to confront someone like this while speaking, but when I do, the student usually backs off right away. Sometimes they'll test me again, as I figured Alpha would, so I never threaten a consequence I'm not willing or able to make happen.

*　　*　　*

Shortly after confronting someone in front of others, I always find a way to go back to them to say I'm proud of the way they responded. I never want to shame them, and affirming them shows it wasn't personal. But it took Alpha less than a minute to test me again. And this time, *he* tried to make it personal.

He turned to his girlfriend and almost shouted, "This guy's lame!" She laughed, but more nervously than before.

This was the money moment. I knew what I did next would either earn everyone's respect, or undermine it, and that ignoring it would bring bigger and more relentless problems.

Sociologists use the term "broken window" to describe a theory of how communities descend into crime and antisocial behavior. It says if a broken window is left unrepaired, it gives the impression no one cares and that vandalism goes unnoticed, so before long all the windows will get broken. The idea is once lesser crimes are tolerated, larger crimes start taking place. Small disorder eventually leads to major disorder.

The theory says the reverse is also true.

New York City Mayor Giuliani believed this, so after being elected in 1994, he implemented zero tolerance for minor crimes like subway fare dodging, public drinking, public urination, graffiti, and the squeegee men who washed windshields at red lights then demanded payment. People complained he was ignoring bigger crimes by putting resources into small ones, but a 2001 study showed that *both* small and serious crime in the city fell suddenly and significantly, and continued to drop for years.

I've seen things work the same way with respect and teenagers. So when Alpha tested me a second time, I looked toward the crowd and said, "I'm sorry we've been interrupted again. This'll only take another minute and we'll get back to Joe."

I lowered the mic and did my best to sound calm, "You didn't believe what I said, and that's okay. But I meant it. I'm not going to let anyone get in the way of what we're doing, so get up and go stand over there with the teachers."

I turned to the principal and said, "If he keeps being distracting over there, you can take him out. But if he's quiet, I want him to stay and be part of everything."

The principal nodded.

As I turned back to Alpha, the awkward silence hung thick with tension. I used to dread these moments, even with my own kids at home, because they feel so counterintuitive, like

I'm ruining the chance for anything positive. But I've learned to trust what students have taught me, and seen amazing things happen as a result of taking a stand. So I said, "Go on over; I'm not going to back down on this."

He sat forward and I felt like I was standing alone on an ice drift and had just poked a polar bear with a number two pencil.

What happened next was like one of my Clint Eastwood fantasies. I looked toward the principal for backup and a guy wearing a yellow security jacket magically appeared, as if from the cinderblock walls, and moved toward us.

He was about forty and of such massive proportions he made Alpha look like Smurfette. His legs were so muscle bound that in the slow motion of that moment the only sound in the gym came from the denim rubbing together on the inside of his thighs. If he'd been wearing corduroy there would have been a small fire.

His expression was calm as he said, "Come on Jake."

Alpha stood, gave me a hard look and followed the guy. Everybody watched, and when they got to the wall, Jake leaned against it at an angle so his side faced me. He looked down to make it clear he wasn't going to listen to a word I said.

Phew.

I turned back to the crowd and said, "Sorry about that, but this way we'll be able to get more done." I tried to sound like it hadn't been a big deal and picked up Joe's story where I'd left off. In the past I'd made the mistake of re-explaining the reasons for what I'd done, but I think that made me look defensive and came across like nagging. Teenagers are smart, and nagging never works. My actions had been enough.

It took a minute or so, but the tension was washed from the

air and the students reengaged and were listening and laughing as if nothing had happened.

In some ways blatant disrespect is simpler to deal with than the subtler testing of my own kids at home, where it can be so understated it's hard to pin down. Maybe it's a passing face expression, a hint of sarcasm or a slight roll of their eyes. It's often so elusive that when I call them on it and they innocently say, "What?" I second-guess myself for bringing it up, even though it feels like I've been slapped in the face.

But disrespect is disrespect, and people like Alpha have taught me it's as damaging to our relationship with teenagers as rust is to a classic car. If we don't deal with it as it surfaces, it will corrode any hope of beauty.

As I moved deeper into Joe's story, I was saying that hiding our pain doesn't work, and that it's never too late to turn things around. I happened to glance at Alpha and he was looking at me over his shoulder and listening. When our eyes met, he looked down again.

During the final ten minutes or so, he turned, the anger gone from his expression, and listened till the end. After I wrapped things up I turned toward him and in a short sentence said I was proud of the way he'd handled himself, then quickly thanked the crowd and everyone clapped. The principal came over and started making announcements, so I went and leaned against the wall beside him.

What happened next is the reason I'm telling you his story. I think about it almost every time I'm tempted to ignore disrespect.

As soon as my back touched the cinderblocks, he came at me. I flinched as he threw his arms over my shoulders, but he buried his face in the nape of my neck and began to sob without shame. The weight of his arms felt like I imagine it would feel to hold a python. I hugged him as best I could and his muffled voice was saying he was just like Joe and wanted to live a better story.

We moved into the hallway, sat shoulder to shoulder on the floor, and he did what he'd never done before. He broke the seal of his hidden past, spilling his loneliness and the fear of his dad on the floor between us. There was no flexing or posturing, just a kid in a giant's body being real.

As I listened I knew he'd need long-term support because he lived alone with his father who was an out-of-work carpenter with substance abuse problems. The first time the alcohol and methamphetamine had spilled over into physical abuse was when Jake was six, and it had never stopped. I got his permission, and found his favorite teacher who came and sat with us on the floor. I watched as Jake told his story again, and could see the teacher was a good man.

When I stood to go, Jake hugged me again and said he was sorry he'd been a jerk. I told him I was proud of his courage and he should keep being honest with his teacher. They both nodded.

When I got to my car, someone called from across the lot and I turned to see Jake's girlfriend running toward me. She had tears and said, "People don't understand. He's got a lot inside no one knows."

I said I thought he was going to be okay now he wasn't trying to handle things on his own. She thanked me and ran back toward the gym.

About ten minutes later I was biting into my grilled cheese

and still amazed at how consistent teenagers are in their need to feel safe. Then my mind drifted and I found myself wondering if Clint ever eats at Denny's.

09

They Need to Live Inside a Great Story

It felt like I'd wandered through the wrong door and stumbled onto a large support group for teenagers with multiple personality disorders.

They'd been one of the mellowest groups I'd seen. There were 2400 of them quietly packed into bleachers and spilling onto the floor. It felt more like a library full of old people than a gym full of teenagers.

I was welcomed with polite applause, and chose a kid at random to bring up front. Friendly banter with one of their own can do a lot to warm up a crowd.

But then, when everyone saw which guy I'd chosen, they switched. There was a sudden startle and detonation of noise that rocked me, as they all leaped to their feet and began chanting and stomping and drowning out the sound system.

"Joe, Joe, Joe, Joe..." I could feel the vibrations in my chest. WWCD?

Whoever this kid was, he was used to this type of reaction. When he saw me trying to get everyone's attention, he waved his arm and they switched back. The place fell silent, like it was naptime at preschool and they wouldn't get milk and cookies if they didn't quiet down.

He turned to me smiling, and shook my hand.

"My name's Joe."

"Yeah, I gathered. So you're in a boy band or something, right?"

The girls giggled.

"Nope" he had an infectious laugh "you should hear me sing. It's pretty bad."

"I'd love to. Why don't you sing something right now?"

Everyone cheered.

He was smiling. "For real?"

I nodded and they cheered louder.

He held up his hand, and belted out an off-key line from "You've Lost that Loving Feeling." The place went nuts and the girls screamed like Beatles fans in old movies.

"Told you."

This kid was great. We joked for a few minutes, and he was so likable I didn't want to end the conversation. He was confident, but not cocky, and though he was funny, he didn't try to steal the show.

Later, the principal explained Joe was loved because he was kind to everyone, even though he was rated as one of the top athletes in the state, had a 4.35 GPA, and dozens of scholarship offers from universities all over North America.

That was October. The weeks drifted into months and I hadn't thought about him till my phone rang at 1:30 a.m., the following April.

Late night calls come with the territory when you speak to thousands of teenagers each month, especially since Al Gore invented the Internet. They can track anyone down. Put a laptop in their hands and they're like bloodhounds with a touchpad nose.

These calls usually come from someone in pain, and frankly, I wish I had a really smart caller ID that would warn me about the nature of the pain.

"Had argument with boyfriend."

Ignore call.

"Don't know who to take to prom."

Ignore call. Block number.

"Legitimate life/death crisis that can't wait till sun up."

Accept call.

I tried to sound awake. "Hello."

"Tyler?"

I couldn't get my bearings.

"Yea, who's this?"

"It's Joe."

I couldn't place him, and wasn't yet aware this would be a conversation, among a handful of others in my life, I'd replay in my mind many times in the years to come. I can't promise to remember it verbatim, but its rhythms and themes are like the face of an old friend I couldn't draw, but could accurately describe.

"Do you have a minute to talk?"

I looked at the clock. "It's one-thirty so I've got like eight hours."

I chuckled. He didn't.

"Sorry it's so late."

"Oh, I didn't mean it that way. This is fine. But I'm sorry, where do I know you from?"

He said the name of his school, then, "I'm the guy you brought up front."

It all came back. "Joe! Wow! What's going on?"

"I need help. I've screwed everything up."

"Tell me what's happened?"

Silence.

"Joe?"

Nothing.

He had a private number and I figured we had a dropped call.

One more try. "Joe? You there?"

Still nothing, then just as I moved the phone from my ear, I heard something that made me stay on the line. He was in the background trying not to cry.

I found out later he'd been fighting tears for years.

"I know you're there and it's okay. Take your time."

And the dam broke. He cried the messy kind of tears that come from long-suppressed pain. It was a flood of wailing and snot and struggled breathing.

Repeated several times, "It's okay. I'm still here. No rush."

When it finally slowed, he took a deep breath and said, "I'm sorry. I didn't think I'd cry."

"That's okay, sounds like you've needed to for a while."

Labored breathing. "Yeah, maybe."

"Tell me what's going on."

"I don't know where to start. I've just felt alone and empty for so long."

"Your school sure seemed to love you."

"Yeah, but they don't know me. Not really. It's not their fault. I walk around pretending all the time."

"In what way?"

"That I'm happy. That all the stuff I've worked so hard to get makes me happy."

"It doesn't?"

"No. I haven't felt happy for a long time."

"Help me understand. Would you say you've been feeling depressed?"

"No, not that. I just feel fake. I'm grateful for what I have, but it's like something's missing. My dad always says we don't have to be perfect; we just have to try our hardest. He says it a lot. Which is cool I guess. But I always thought things would feel different."

"In what way?"

"I don't know. More satisfying. More significant. Everyone's always saying how cool my life is, but if I'm honest, all the things I've done feel empty. Meaningless even. It feels like there's some huge piece missing I can't figure out. But now I've screwed all that up anyway."

"What do you mean?"

"I don't want to put all this on you."

"No, it's okay. Keep going."

"Well, everyone seems to think if they had my life, they'd love it. So at first, when I started winning awards and stuff, I was surprised when it didn't feel like I thought it would. They'd pat me on the back or whatever, and I'd smile, but inside it never felt meaningful... Sorry, I'm repeating myself."

"It's okay. So how long have you been feeling like this?"

"I guess it started when I was a freshman. I tried to ignore it. Then last year I won this big award, and even that didn't mean much. I remember looking around at everyone thinking we're all chasing stupid stuff... I don't know, is this making sense?"

"Yea it is."

"So around Christmas I started doing something stupid. I

was looking for food and opened the cabinet above the fridge. My dad keeps alcohol up there. He never drinks unless there's a party, and I don't think he's had one since my mom died."

"I'm sorry Joe."

"Thanks."

"When did she pass away?"

"Almost five years ago."

"That must be hard. Do you think her being gone is why you feel like this?"

"I don't think so. I think it'd feel this way even if she was here. My aunt's been there for me, but I don't know."

"So I'm guessing you had some of your dad's liquor."

"Yeah. I never drank before. It just never appealed to me. But I thought 'Why not?' If I'm honest, the idea of it felt exciting. Like it might help. So I had some Vodka."

"And did your dad find out?"

"Not then. But it helped me feel less numb. Or maybe more numb, I don't know. All I knew was it helped. So I did it again a few more times, then got a bottle from this kid at school and before long I was drinking almost every day. I only did it alone at home, because my coach has rules where he kicks guys off the team for drinking, and spring football was coming."

"So how long did this go on?"

"Well I got away with it for months. I promised myself I'd only do it till spring practices started, so most days I'd come home and sit here on my bed and drink till I fell asleep. My dad works nights, but a few weeks ago he came home to get something and caught me. I was pretty wasted."

"What'd he say?"

"He freaked out. I don't remember much, but the next

morning he was yelling saying he'd never trust me again. He's still pretty disappointed in me. We never talked much before, but hardly at all now."

"So is that what you meant when you said you'd screwed things up?"

"Well it's part of it."

He was choked up again.

"I kept drinking and somehow Coach found out and told me I couldn't play spring ball. The truth is I respect him for it, but it was a big deal because I hadn't chosen a college yet, so a lot of them were sending reps to watch me play so we could talk. They found out why I was off the team and I lost my scholarships."

I could tell he was on the edge of tears again.

"No wonder you're overwhelmed."

His voice was shaking, "Things felt empty before, but now it's like the perfect storm and I'm not strong enough..."

His words trailed off and he started to cry, but managed, "There's something else."

"Okay."

Something in his voice changed. "I wasn't going to tell you."

He blew out a deep breath and when he spoke, his voice grew softer with each word.

"I've got my dad's twenty-two pistol on the bed next to me. I'm falling apart..."

More sobbing.

"I'm glad you told me. We'll get you through this, just stay on the line, okay?"

"Okay."

I remember what it feels like to be suicidal. It's as if you're looking through a long tube that's pointed at your pain. Your other eye is closed, so your pain is all you see, and it feels like nothing could ever make it go away. You need help to pull the tube away so you can see there's more, that there's hope, because you can't do it yourself.

We talked for about an hour, and I mostly listened. His intelligence was causing him to ask the big questions. He wondered about suffering in the world, and all the war, and why his rich uncle always needed something newer and shinier, and how the kids at school thought they'd be happier if they had this thing or that, and how empty the pursuit of happiness felt, and it all kept bringing him back to the ultimate question about the meaning of his own life.

His dad was distant, his Mom was gone, and his teachers couldn't see what he didn't show, so he'd been searching for answers alone. The troubled waters below his smooth surface had led him to despair, and then self-destruction.

Joe had been living the best story he knew how, but the Teenage American Dream of popularity, success in sports, perfect grades, and big-time scholarships wasn't enough. In the end, those things never are. They're the myths we tell each other to make ourselves feel better in our search for meaning.

*   *   *

Our conversation took a good turn when I told him about a student named Blake I'd met. I said he also wanted to live inside a better story.

Blake went to college on a tennis scholarship then started some businesses, but found his better story when he was traveling in Argentina and saw how hard life was for kids without shoes. Some of them were catching diseases and even dying. He had a simple idea. He thought if he could start a small shoe company, maybe they could give one pair away in the developing world for every pair they sold at home. "One for One," he thought.

He named his company TOMS Shoes, and now since he had the idea in 2006, they've delivered over ten million shoes to kids in forty countries.

I told Joe Blake's business card doesn't read, "CEO, TOMS Shoes" but "Chief Shoe Giver." I said I think the best stories are ones that have to do with life and death and I thought Blake was living inside a really great one. Blake didn't give up the American Dream, he just found a more meaningful path to it.

*   *   *

Something clicked inside Joe. He said it never occurred to him before, but all the things he'd worked so hard at were self-focused. He said they were valuable in their own way, but maybe they hadn't been enough because they only benefitted him. He said maybe if he started doing something for others, his life would have more meaning, like Blake's.

I agreed and said I don't think we find happiness by pursuing it, but by using parts of our lives to help other people who are hurting.

While we talked he locked the gun back in his dad's closet and we did a conference call to his best friend. I stayed on the line till his friend came over to spend the rest of the night with him.

His friend said he had no idea Joe was in any pain, and Joe said maybe they could find something to do together to help others.

The tube was coming away from his eye.

"Thanks for talking Tyler. Do you think it'd be okay if I called again tomorrow?"

"That'd be great. Call anytime."

*   *   *

I'll tell you the end of Joe's story in a second, but first want to mention a dad who had a great relationship with his daughter till she turned fourteen and started hanging out with a boy who was bad news.

She started wearing all black, just like him, listening to his heavy metal music and being disrespectful. In the evenings she used to tell her dad about her day, but now it was hard to get her to take her ear buds out, even at dinner. She'd changed so fast he didn't know what to do and neither did his wife.

He wanted her to stop seeing the boy, but anytime he talked about it she got mad and slammed her bedroom door. He missed her and was afraid of pushing her away, so he backed off.

Then one day at work he had a thought. *Maybe this boy is just the best story she knows how to live right now, and maybe we can give her a chance to find a better one.*

So he did some research and went home and told his family they were all going to raise money for an orphanage in Mexico where kids lived in a dump and were dying of diseases. He said they'd all have to pitch in.

His son liked the idea and said he'd sell lemonade and do odd jobs, but it didn't go so well with his daughter. She got mad, said it was stupid and slammed her door again. He told his wife and son they were going to do it anyway.

Weeks went by and they were raising money, but the daughter just listened to her music. It seemed hopeless till she burst into their room one night and jumped onto their bed holding her phone without the ear buds.

She said she thought she could raise money online, and they had to go to Mexico right away so she could take pictures of the dump and the actual kids they were going to help. Her dad said okay, and the next day they skipped school and work and drove to Mexico.

On the way home she told her dad from the back seat she'd broken up with the boy because he was a jerk and told her to lose weight.

She'd found a better story, he had his daughter back, and they helped a lot of orphans.[1]

*   *   *

I think sometimes we're so focused on keeping teenagers away from risky behavior, we've forgotten that the thing inside them that pulls them toward danger is a healthy longing to live an *adventure*. Not the fake kind they get in video games

---

[1] Donald Miller told this true story about the dad, the girl and the orphanage, in a speech given at Mars Hill Church in Grandville, Michigan on 11/11/07.

and amusement parks, but the life-and-death kind where they do something important that helps lessen the suffering in other people's stories, where they get to live for something bigger than themselves.

I have a friend who took his family to live in Costa Rica for a year, just for the adventure. They're helping people there, and I think he's a really smart dad because he wants his kids to see they're made for something more than comfort and consuming.

I can't afford to move to Costa Rica for a year, but I wonder sometimes if I'm showing my kids how they can find meaning and joy here, in the midst of our daily lives with hurting people all around us.

I think the best way I can show them is by living a great story myself. And then, like St. Francis of Assisi says, when all else fails, I should use words.

*   *   *

Joe found his story. He started with baby steps, then after graduation, joined the army where he could help protect justice and freedom, like his grandfather had. In the years that followed, he was selected for training in the U.S. Special Forces, where today he's a valued member of the Green Beret.

But he still can't sing.

10

They Need More Than Love

Because of what I've learned from teenagers like Joe, Moema and others, I'm often asked to spend time with teachers or families who are struggling.

That's what brought me to Linda and Rob's house. It was a late Friday afternoon, and the sunshine was conspiring with the breeze to make it difficult to go inside.

*   *   *

"I'm sorry, Rob's in traffic but should be here in a couple minutes."

She was leading me to the kitchen where three glasses of lemonade waited on the island, sparkling in the sun. Drops of condensation clung to them like little jewels. As we sat opposite each other, I noticed a pair of scissors lying on the black granite countertop in front of her. The sun flashed off their blade as I took my stool.

There was a pause so I said, "Danville's always been one of my favorite towns in the Bay Area."

Linda was built like a track star, with long limbs and dark hair pulled back into a ponytail. Her eyes were deep and intelligent but softened by sadness, and she wasn't into small talk. This was a relief since I'm not very good at it.

"We love it here. Thanks for being willing to come talk. It means a lot since we're out of ideas with our daughter."

"Tell me more."

She tucked her legs under her stool. "Her name's Heather, and last Friday we were..."

She shifted and one of her thumbs began rubbing circles over the knuckles on her other hand.

"...It's embarrassing but I was chasing her around this island with these scissors like some crazy person, screaming at the top of my lungs. She's fourteen but wants to dress like a twenty-five-year-old stripper."

Her hand absentmindedly slid the scissors away.

"Heather was about to leave for school and we were upstairs. I said she couldn't wear the top she had on and she said she didn't care what I wanted and turned to walk away. I told her not to turn her back but she kept going so I went after her. We ended up down here and I grabbed the scissors thinking it would show how serious I was and I started yelling I was going to cut it off!"

I've since learned Linda's not prone to outbursts, and think most of us would be surprised if we knew how many of us have done things like this. We just don't talk about them at dinner parties.

"So did you get it? Did you cut it off?"

My question pulled her from the memory. "Oh, um, no, she's too fast."

"Maybe next time you should trip her on the stairs."

She laughed and I could tell she was relieved I wasn't going to judge her, then her smile faded and her eyes looked sad again. "We feel like we've lost her. Like maybe it's too late."

I was about to say how hard that must be when Rob pushed open the screen door. He was tall, had vibrant eyes set below a strong brow and a full head of thick hair dusted with premature grey, and was wearing surgical scrubs.

I could tell he didn't want to be there.

I knew this because he's a man.

Most of us men aren't thrilled when our wife sets up an appointment for us to get advice from a stranger. It feels like we're being called a failure and told the stranger is smarter. If I were Rob I might have called with a pretend flat tire and taken a nap under some tree.

We shook hands and he sat next to Linda and looked at the scissors.

"So she told you?"

I nodded "Yeah."

They were both quiet so I said, "I know you just sat down, but would it be okay if we went for a walk while we all talk? I've been inside all day."

Rob looked relieved and said he wanted to throw on some shorts. While we waited Linda mentioned Heather was away for the weekend with her church, and I thought the preacher should mention strippers don't usually get chosen prom queen.

*   *   *

The reason I wanted to walk and talk wasn't just that I like being outside. It was also because I read some research that proves males feel most comfortable talking shoulder to shoulder. It helps us open up. In our brain, face-to-face can feel confrontational. This is opposite to how the research showed female minds work. Women tend to face each other for intimate conversation and turn away when they're mad.

Linda was already opening up to me, and I thought walking might give Rob the best chance to do the same.

I was skeptical about the research at first, but the morning I read it I showed up at a school before the first bell and noticed most girls were standing or sitting in circles, and most guys were leaning against walls, side by side. I used to think boys did this just to check girls out, which they do, but I realized there's more to it since most meaningful conversations I've had with my sons were in a car, sitting shoulder to shoulder. [2]

*   *   *

I was tempted to tell Rob about the research so he'd think I was smart, but remembered he's a surgeon so I was in over my head.

When we got to the street it was clear he wasn't into small talk either, which is probably good in a guy who cuts people open and puts his hands inside. You'd want a guy like that to get right to the point.

"To be honest," he said, "I can't blame Linda for the scissors. I've been avoiding Heather for the last few months because I'm afraid I'll say or do something I regret. Most days I drive home and wish I could trade lives with the neighbors up the street, since their teenagers seem great."

Linda mentioned things had been fine till Heather reached

---

[2] Deborah Tannen, Gender and Discourse (New York: Oxford University Press, 1994), p. 94ff. I've included this information because it's the reason I sat shoulder to shoulder with Alpha in the hall and Josiah in the bleachers, but was face to face with Moema under that tree and with Keiko at her Catholic School. It's revolutionized how Kristen and I talk to our kids and each other, especially during moments of tension.

puberty and began liking boys. I started to say all boys are demon possessed and we should keep our daughters away when someone shouted from a front porch, "Hi you guys."

It was a family of five, they were good looking and I knew they were the neighbors Rob had been talking about. Mom, dad and three teenagers were sitting around a table eating dinner; sweet happiness dripping from their silverware. I assumed they smelled good too.

"Wanna come up for some salad?"

Salad! I've never trusted people who eat salad on Friday nights.

Rob sounded sincere, "We're just out for a walk. But thanks anyway!"

Then under his breath, "Can you see why I hate them?"

I mumbled, "Yeah, I bet those aren't even their real kids. I'm guessing Craigslist." Then I looked at their mailbox to see if it said Stepford.

We waved good-bye and as we walked on, Rob and Linda took turns telling stories. After about thirty minutes it was getting cool so we turned back. As we passed the Stepford house again, Rob was staring at it and I could see he was deep in thought. About fifty feet later he nodded back toward it and asked an important question.

"We love Heather as much as they love their kids, so how come I never hear yelling from their house when ours is full of it?"

He was looking at me now like I was the surgeon and he was a desperate patient.

"What are they doing that we're not?"

I could feel the weight of what was at stake for them, and wished I had a smart answer practiced and ready. But then the seeds of a fresh idea popped into my mind so I said it with fake confidence, like Freud and I'd been discussing it over wiener schnitzels that morning.

I stopped walking and pointed back at the Stepford house "We're walking away from their home and toward yours, right?"

"Yeah?"

The smart part was apparently taking its time to come out.

"Let's say every step we take with our feet represents one parenting choice."

"Okay."

"And that good choices take us toward the happier home, but choices that aren't the best take us toward the less happy one."

Linda said, "I see what you're saying but the problem with that is we've always made our choices out of love. Never for ourselves."

"I know you have. It's obvious how much you love her. And that's what's tricky about all this. How much we love someone isn't what determines which way our choices take the relationship. What matters are the beliefs that lie behind our choices, because those beliefs determine whether our choices will be good or not."

I thought of my own story. "I can look back over my life and see that every bad choice I've ever made grew out of confused or wrong beliefs about what mattered. I've never wanted to mess things up, but the choices that brought the most pain all grew out of believing the wrong things."

I thought of something my dad told me once, "We all make the choices we do based on what we believe will make us happy. Even the guy in jail who stole computers to get cash for drugs believed stealing would make him happier. He was just wrong about what he believed."

Rob pointed at the Stepford house and without sounding

defensive said, "So you're saying they believe right things, and we don't?"

"I don't know what they believe, or even if they really are happy, but if they have great relationships with their kids, then enough of their parenting choices are based on right beliefs about how to relate to their kids."

No one spoke for a moment and my mind was racing because I know some parents make great choices, and their kids still end up making bad ones. But there were some things Linda and Rob had said while we were walking that made me suspect they had some child-centered ideas.

I broke the silence "Do you remember when Michael Jackson first moonwalked on that awards show years ago?"

Linda nodded and Rob said, "Yeah, kind of. I was a little kid."

It's unsettling when doctors are younger than you.

"Well I was in graduate school and the next day everyone was trying to moonwalk. Even white guys like me. I guess my point is most parents I meet who're having a hard time love their kids a lot and have been facing the happy home the whole time. But they've been doing this."

I turned to face the Stepford home. "All of us are looking this way. *We all want the happy home, and have been doing everything we can to move toward it. But if we believe the wrong things about our role in kids' lives, then even though we love them, we'll be moonwalking. Facing the right way, but moving backward.*"

I didn't want to distract them by trying to moonwalk, so I just took small steps backward. "And it's usually not obvious which way we've been moving till our kids hit puberty."

Linda's heart was still heavy. "So do you think it's too late for us with Heather?"

"No, absolutely not. I've seen families facing unbelievable rebellion turn things around, and I feel extra hope for you guys because you're both being so honest. You'd be surprised how many parents just want to talk about what's wrong with their kids, but aren't willing to look at themselves."

Rob said, "At this point we're willing to do whatever it takes."

I think their pain was a gift in that moment because it had prepared them to think differently.

We walked again and as we were getting near their house Rob asked if I'd stay longer if he threw some steaks on the grill.

Steaks! This guy really was smart.

*   *   *

As we ate, they explained one of their most relentless struggles with Heather was homework. She'd say she finished it at school or didn't have any, but she was falling behind. They'd made a rule homework had to be done right after school, even on Fridays because of a pattern of procrastination on weekends. They said they'd made a big deal about this.

Then Linda told a simple story about a fight they'd had months earlier. It had been the tipping point that marked the day Heather began closing them out completely. As it turned out, Linda's story shed a lot of light on things.

*   *   *

Heather had been withdrawing from them in the normal ways a new teenager needs to. They'd always anticipated it, but when it happened, the loss was visceral and felt worse than expected.

Heather had asked to go to a friend's pool party right after school on a Friday, saying it was a big deal and everyone would be there. Linda knew there was a project due Monday and asked how much was left to do, and Heather said, "Not much." So to avoid a fight she let Heather go, but insisted she finish the project the next day.

Heather got excited and even kissed her, and the affection was like water in a desert. That evening Rob had the idea they could maybe reconnect with Heather if they spent Saturday as a family before he left on the redeye Saturday night. They figured she'd go for it if they took her to San Francisco and promised to go to the Cirque Du Soleil show she'd wanted to see.

Heather got home and was excited about Cirque and Linda said she'd help with the project on Sunday.

So they all headed to San Francisco the next morning and had a great time. But then on Sunday, Linda forgot she'd promised to spend the day with her sister who was going through a divorce. She told Heather she wouldn't be able to help with the project, and Heather got mad.

"That's not fair! You promised!!"

Linda explained sometimes things happen in life we have to roll with, but Heather didn't want a lecture. She just slammed her door.

When Linda got home that evening, Heather was still mad and yelled, "This stupid project is hard and if I fail it's your fault!"

Linda tried to talk but Heather wouldn't let her. "You always lecture me about commitments, but *you* don't even keep them! You yell about homework but won't help and now I'm screwed! I hate you!"

Slam.

*   *   *

I thought it would help so I told them about a summer job I had in college painting dorm buildings, and how one day I was getting water from the cooler and the foreman came over and we talked for fifteen minutes about how we loved Robin Williams in this TV show called *Mork and Mindy*.

I walked away thinking my boss was pretty cool.

A couple days later, I'd just come up to the cooler with another worker and the boss laid into us for wasting time and yelled we should get back to work.

I walked away thinking he was moody.

Then the next week, he and I talked about *Mork and Mindy* at the cooler again for a long time, and I walked away thinking he was a jerk.

I told Linda and Rob his rules felt arbitrary and based on his mood, and his lectures felt like personal attacks because he was a hypocrite. I said a lot of kids who confide in me say that's how their parents make them feel.

Linda said, "I can see why she's so angry."

The cool thing was they didn't defend themselves but asked lots of questions. This meant we were able to talk about things that can be hard to hear when your kid has hurt you.

Things like how it's a mistake to flex on rules just to avoid a fight because it makes us look weak. And how weakness makes Heather feel unsafe since she's not done on the inside. We even talked about how Giuliani used the broken window theory in New York and how inconsistency looks like a broken window to Heather, and pretty soon she wants to break all the windows.

I suggested Heather wore that top because it made her feel powerful in the world of her peers, but what she needed was to have serious consequences because she'd disrespected them about it.

*   *   *

They walked me to my car and asked if there was any chance we could talk again. Linda said, "We know we need to talk to her about all this, but don't know how to get her to sit down for a conversation."

Rob smiled, "If you like rack of lamb with garlic mashed potatoes, that's what we're having tomorrow night."

"I love rack of lamb! In fact, I also love seared Ahi and fresh fruit smoothies and grilled cheese with tomato soup and chocolate malts, and I hope Heather stays rebellious for a long time."

They laughed. "Just promise you'll never write about us in some book."

"I promise."

*   *   *

The next evening on their patio, between bites of lamb and potato, I told them how an old lady rescued me, and how she said something that helps every time I need to get a teenager to listen; even when it's my own son.

11

They Have a Reset Button
(How to Have the Conversation)

There was something about the unknowns of what lay ahead that thrilled me. I couldn't stop smiling.

The tassel had been turned, I'd hugged my college friends and family good-bye, and San Francisco was waiting on the other side of the country. I turned Queen up on my in-dash cassette player and pictured myself sitting by the bay in the California sun creating lesson plans that would shape hundreds of young minds.

I was educated, full of hope; Freddie Mercury was singing "Don't Stop Me Now"; and my brain was awash with dopamine.

But then, only weeks after school started, my neurotransmitters stopped carrying the pleasure hormone and I was drowning in stress.

I'd been wrong to think working with kids was my gift. I felt trapped, hopeless, and for the first time in my life, couldn't sleep. There was one thing in particular that chewed at me during the dark hours as I tossed and kicked at the sheets.

It was Dolores.

Her success just didn't make sense.

She had many of the same students I had, was the oldest teacher on staff and nearing retirement, was small, wore no makeup, was fussy about neatness, notorious for the amount of work she demanded, dressed like an Amish grandmother and even her name was obsolete, yet her students, who lived in the shadow of one of the most progressive cities in the world, adored and respected her.

In contrast, I was tall, young, fresh out of college with the latest teaching techniques, understood popular culture, was the head soccer coach, and even drove a really cool white 1972 Corvette, yet I was struggling with disrespect from my students, and especially in my tenth grade lit class.

I dreaded those sophomores every morning, and felt defeated every afternoon as I watched them walk out at the end of fifth period. I cared about them, but no longer liked them and knew they didn't like me much either. My best hadn't been good enough so during winter break I made the decision to quit teaching altogether.

*   *   *

Years later I felt a similar despair, but this time it was far more personal. Being in the same room or car with my own son Paul had become a struggle. He was fourteen and every strand of my DNA longed to feel close to him, but negativity had built a frustrating barrier between us and nothing I tried made any difference.

It empties you when love can't find a way to gain respect.

*   *   *

Dolores had always shown me kindness. She'd been the first

to invite me to sit with her in the teacher's room during lunch, had said she was there if I needed anything, and even checked to make sure I had somewhere to spend Christmas. She seemed genuinely happy for me when I said I did.

I called her on New Year's day because I didn't want her to hear I was quitting from someone else. As I explained my reasons, she listened without judgment then asked if I liked ice cream. A half hour later I was sipping a chocolate malt and listening to her talk, between bites from her child's cup of vanilla, about how much she loved the track.

"You mean the horse track?"

"Yup."

"You bet on the ponies?"

"Yup."

"Really?"

"Uh-huh."

Definitely not Amish.

"Wow."

"I mainly love being around the horses."

"Hm."

"Ever see a thoroughbred up close?"

"Nope."

"Magnificent. They weigh a thousand pounds. Pure muscle."

"That big?"

"Yup. And their eyes are wild!"

"Never would've guessed you'd be into that."

"I love it."

"That's cool."

"Know what else I'm into?"

"Drinking?"

"Don't be ridiculous."

"Then I can't imagine."

"I'm into you."

I smiled. "Quit messing with me."

"Not in the way you're thinking Dear."

"Come on. You know you want me."

She rocked her head back and giggled.

It was infectious.

While she wiped her eyes she said, "Sometime I'll tell you about the one true love of my life."

"I'd love to meet him."

"Thank you Sweetie, but he's been gone a long time now."

I should have known.

"I'm sorry."

"Don't be. Ben gave me enough happiness during our twelve years to last forever. I'm still full of it."

Something faraway in her smile told me she was back there with him for a moment. I should have let her stay but was clumsy. "I'd love to hear the story."

Her eyes refocused. "And I'd love to tell it."

Then she straightened in her chair and said, "But I want to talk about your story. When I say I'm into you, I mean your future. It's going to be fun to watch."

"I wish I knew what to do."

"I think you're going to be a great teacher."

"Thanks, but I'm thinking something with cars."

"I've seen that fancy Camaro of yours."

"Corvette, actually."

"Don't be picky Dear."

"Sorry."

"Whatever it is, it's pretty..."

"Corvette."

She ignored me.

"... but I think teaching is your thing."

"Well, you've never watched me during fifth period."

"Doesn't matter."

"I think it does."

"Nope. You could grow to love those kids again."

"Well maybe, but I don't know if I want to. And anyway, I think they deserve a better teacher."

"You said they were disrespectful."

"Yup."

"I don't think respect is your problem."

"Well you can't teach when a few jerks control the room."

"That's true. That's why we have to be in control of the class."

"I tried."

She tilted her head. "Is it okay if I give you a little advice?"

"Um, sure. Of course!"

"Kids are like my horses at the track. Those animals don't run because the little men on their backs make them. They'd run on their own if you let them; they're bred for it. But they're squirrely so they need the jockey to guide them."

"Sounds easier than teaching 'cause they get to use a whip."

"It's called a riding crop Dear, and modern ones don't hurt, they just make noise. And anyway the rider gives cues mostly with his voice and small touches that position the horse and tell it when to go all-out at the finish."

"Didn't know that."

"And you know the reason such a huge animal gives a hundred-pound man control over all that power?"

"No."

"Because it trusts him."

"So you're saying my students don't trust me?"

"Yes."

"Did they tell you?"

"Didn't have to."

"So how do you know?"

"Any room full of teenagers is more powerful than a horse, and like the thoroughbred, when they trust us, they'll let us lead them anywhere."

"Those jockeys only weigh a hundred pounds?"

"Focus Dear."

"Sorry."

"If they don't trust us, they won't respect us. But when they do, the respect follows."

"Sounds all tidy when you say it, but I had their trust at first and they were still disrespectful."

"How could you have their trust when they didn't know you yet? They don't give it for free because of our position. They want to trust us, but we have to earn and demand it."

"And that's the point. I'm not gifted like you."

"It's not about gifting."

She drew a long breath. "How about this, you try something for me, and if it doesn't work, you quit and we'll jump in that Camaro of yours and go watch the ponies."

"Corvette."

She smiled. "Please let that go Dear."

And for the next ten minutes she poured out her wisdom. Some of it spilled onto the table and was lost, but what soaked in was enough to transform how I relate to kids. It helped me build the trust my classes needed in order to respect me, and changed the trajectory of my career. And though I didn't know it at the time, years later it would breathe life into my relationship with Paul.

*   *   *

"You need to walk into class the first day back from vacation and have an honest conversation with them."

I was way ahead of her. I'd heard it before. I needed to tell them they owed me an apology and they should take responsibility for their behavior. But then her next words shocked me.

"You need to apologize to them and take responsibility for how things are."

I was shocked. "Me apologize? For what?"

My mind was racing. "That'll make me look weak."

She smiled. "From what you tell me they already think you're weak. And this isn't about seeking their approval. It's about being a decent person who cares enough to be honest."

"But why is it my fault?"

"Because you're the adult."

"But they don't listen. They don't even like me."

"And you've made it clear you don't like them either. Yes?"

"Yes."

"And why should they listen when you've allowed it to get personal and they know you don't like them?"

I'd never thought about it like that before.

"But I literally can't even get my fifth period to be quiet long enough to listen."

"I bet you a half gallon of vanilla ice cream you can."

"I think you have a gambling problem."

She ignored me again, which is a classic attribute of addiction.

"Here's how you do it. You stand up and say *there's something you need to ask them to forgive you for. Then you let the words hang there. They'll quiet down. Then say it again and they might even lean forward and hold their breath because they won't want to miss what you're about to say.*"

"But what do I apologize for? Don't they owe me an apology?"

"No. It's your responsibility to set the tone in your relationship with them, not theirs."

"I don't understand."

"Tell them you're sorry you've allowed them to be disrespectful to you and each other, and that it's not their fault, it's yours. Tell them you understand why they would have a hard time trusting you about things you say are important, like respect, when you haven't backed them up with your actions. Admit you forgot your job is to be an adult who expects great and high things from them."

"I don't think most of them think of me as an adult. Some of the girls are dating guys older than me."

"It's not about your age. It's about your role in their life. But you've got to be honest about things. Like how you've blamed them for making the class hard to manage. You should even tell them you were thinking of quitting until you realized none of this has been their fault. Make it clear it's been yours. The more real you are the better."

"What if it doesn't work?"

"It will. Remember they're just little kids in teenage bodies who want adults to take a stand on what matters, and back it up."

"But how do I back it up?"

"You tell them you're going to expect better things from them, and you're going to change how you respond when they test you. Be specific about things like getting seated and facing front and raising their hands and taking notes and handing in homework. But there's something you have to remember the whole time."

"That I'm scared of them?"

"You must've driven your mother crazy! *Remember to expect them to test you. So tell them right up front that when they do, you won't take it personally. Tell them you understand that testing is the only way they can find out if you mean what you say, so it won't hurt your feelings. Then tell them you'll do your best to follow through every time because they deserve to be part of a class where good things are happening.*"

"And exactly what do I do when they test me?"

"You give them a consequence. A lot of teachers just send kids to the office, like it's the administrator's job to fix them. Don't do that. Tell them you'll give them in-lunch detention in your classroom. Or tell them you'll make them stay after school in your room, even if it means they'll miss the bus and their parents will have to come get them, or they'll miss the beginning of sports practice or whatever. They hate losing their freedom."

"But all I'll be doing is writing detention slips."

"At first it will feel that way, but it'll get better once they know they can trust the things you say."

"They're going to hate me."

"Maybe at first."

"Great!"

"But most will respect that you're willing to take a stand, especially when they see you follow through. Kids want us to expect a lot from them; they just don't know it. It shows we trust their ability to do more than they think they can. There'll always be a few jerks, but eventually even they'll catch on."

"But I don't think my classroom is big enough to fit everyone I'll have to give slips to."

"You'll only need to hand out a few and the other kids will see you're serious."

"I'll never remember all this."

She took out a pen and slid it across the table with a napkin.

"Write these six things down, then memorize them like something you expect your soccer players to remember to score a touchdown."

"There're no touchdowns in soccer."

"You're being picky again!"

*   *   *

As I write to you I regret losing that napkin through the years. But I devoted myself to her advice and believe what follows is very close to what she said.

*   *   *

"Write down, 'How to Press the Reset Button.'"

I jotted it down.

"No, at the top. Here's another napkin, and write more neatly."

I smiled and wrote it.

"Okay, *1. Begin by saying you need to ask them to forgive you for something."*

She was watching me.

"Write a bit faster Dear, but keep it neat."

"Sorry."

"*2. Apologize: Admit you've allowed them to disrespect you and each other, and it isn't their fault, it's yours, and you want them to forgive you.*"

She said I had to own my apology. Even though they were wrong to act the way they had, my apology shouldn't sound like I was blaming them at the same time. She said to take responsibility because the goal was to reset my relationship so they'd see me as an adult who expects a lot for the sake of their future.

"Do you think they'll believe me?"

"Yes I do. *3. Tell them you're going to change how you respond when they test you, then give specific examples.*"

"Like what?"

"Anything you want them to change. Like, if they talk without raising their hand, they'll get lunch detention and have to eat in your room in silence. Or if they distract the class in any way they'll get after-school detention."

"How many examples should I give?"

"Just a couple. They're smart. Just say you're talking about all the things they already know about how to act in class. If you give a long list you'll sound like you're nagging. *Nagging and lectures don't work with teenagers. Consequences do.*"

I wrote that down too.

"*4. Tell them you expect them to test you, and you won't take it personally.*"

"But they're going to make it feel personal."

"If it hurts your feelings just fake it, but remember it's not personal. They need to test because they're human, and you need to follow through because you're the adult."

"Okay."

"Then 5. *Tell them you'll do your best to follow through every time.* Let them know in the beginning it will seem like a lot of slips, but once they see how serious you are, things will settle down and everyone will enjoy class like they deserve to."

My hand was getting tired.

"And 6. *Tell them you want to hear what they think about all this*, and remind them to raise their hand before they speak. *Then listen without defending yourself!*"

"How long should I let them talk?"

"You'll know. They might have questions. Just make them feel heard, and don't defend yourself. *And expect the testing to start right away.*"

"And I'm supposed to give out slips right then if they test me?"

"Write their name on a piece of paper and tell them after class they'll get their slip. *Be strong. The testing is the most important part. It's where the reset button gets pressed because it shows where the new fences are. When they test you, you're going to feel like you've lost and nothing has changed. But you've changed everything!*"

"How'd you get so smart?"

"Good mentors."

"Thanks for all this."

"You're welcome. Try not to let anything slide past, because they'll be watching carefully."

"Sounds like a lot of work."

"It will be at first. But eventually it will make everything easier. My classes are pure joy because I establish what I expect right away."

"Is that why they love you?"

"I think it's my flashy clothes. And yes, love comes with boundaries."

"You really think I can do this?"

"A moron could do this."

She giggled. "And I bet one day you're going to tell me how much you love fifth period."

*   *   *

My heart was thumping as I apologized to my classes, and I fumbled most with my words in fifth period. But it turns out, Dolores was right about everything.

*   *   *

Years later I was alone in the car with Paul and pulled over in an ice-skating rink parking lot. He asked what we were doing, so I turned the engine off and said I needed to ask his forgiveness for something.

My eyes are full as I write because the conversation that followed became the most pivotal moment in our relationship. I followed Dolores' advice verbatim, as I'd done with my students, and it allowed me to press the reset button with Paul in a way that helped us both see what we could expect from each other, without feeling like a "me against you" thing. He's twenty-five now, and a few weeks ago we were grilling steaks, and I started to ask if he remembered the conversation, and he interrupted to say, "You mean the one in the ice-skating rink parking lot?"

I nodded, and as he retold it to me, I smiled and wished I could call Dolores to say thank-you. But she's long since gone to be with her Ben. If it's possible to see the fruit of our lives from heaven, I bet she smiles down on me from time to time, in between poker games with Saint Peter.

*   *   *

It didn't take long for Paul to begin testing me, and I remembered Dolores saying nagging and lectures don't work with teenagers, consequences do. It was hard at first to know what consequences to give. But then I remembered her saying "They love their freedom." That thought, along with an experience I had with a surfer around the same time, led to some very practical answers.

12

They Need True-Points

I stood beneath the Golden Gate trying to ignore the thumping in my chest. The pulse in my ears was almost loud enough to drown out the thunder of the waves crashing into the boulders along the road. The swell was huge and the breakers raged as if some bigger bully had beaten them out at sea, and their impotence there had made them angry and driven them to this spot with the intent to harm.

I was afraid to paddle out.

A dozen of us stood in silence with our boards under our arms watching the water churn, staring at the only one who'd been brave enough to get in the water. When that surfer caught a set wave and timed it perfectly to climb safely out of the water, I went over to ask my question. As I did, her eyes were dripping adrenaline in tempo with the water falling from her hair.

"Aren't you afraid of the rocks?"

"Always." She smiled. "That's why I have true-points."

I had no idea what she was talking about, so I stood a little straighter and nodded toward the waves. "Oh yea, of course, true-points."

"No, over there." She was pointing to the hill behind us. As I turned, our eyes met and her expression told me she knew I'd been pretending to understand.

She smiled but didn't tease. "See that flagpole and tree up there? When the surf's big like today, the current wants to drag you into the rocks. With everything going on it's tough to tell where you are, so once you've paddled to a safe spot, you find two objects on the shore that line up, one behind the other. Then you just keep checking to make sure you haven't drifted. That tree and flagpole keep me safe."

She looked at my board, "You should get out there. It's fun!"

I thanked her then waited till she drove away before I put my board in my truck, grabbed a sandwich from my cooler, and sat down to think about what she'd said.

13

They Keep You From Drifting

Our final two chapters are like the flagpole and tree, because they give us, and the teenagers we care about, something to look at when life wants to pull us into the rocks. They're simple, and so easy to see that Kristen and I wrote them down and hung them on our kitchen wall next to the pencil marks that show how tall we're all getting.

We put them there to remind everyone what we can expect from each other.

14

They Need Freedom

It was twenty-two years ago and I still remember my nerves swirling as I walked through the crisp Canadian air toward the building. Lights glared off a poster by the multipurpose room door reading, "Tyler Durman. Expert on Teenagers." They'd asked me to come speak to parents and teachers for the first time, and though I'd spoken to thousands of students, I felt like anything but an expert.

I was sitting at the end of the first row when the MC welcomed the crowd and I realized I was holding my breath. I tried to let it out slowly so no one would notice.

"Just breathe," I told myself, "This is Canada, where even carjackers are friendly."

When I took the microphone I noticed snow had started falling in slow motion through the lights in the parking lot. It made everything feel surreal, like some sluggish stress-filled dream. I put my hand in a pocket to confirm I'd remembered to wear pants.

I labored through the hour and as I was wrapping up, a dad in the front row raised his hand. I'd noticed him earlier because he'd been so focused all evening he'd hardly moved. He sat like one of those lifelike statues you might find on a mall bench, with his calloused hands resting in his lap and his work boots planted firmly on the floor.

He had a warm voice that carried throughout the room. "My daughter's angry because she wants a boyfriend and I've told her she's not ready. I'm afraid I'm pushing her away and need to know, am I doing the right thing?"

Gulp.

I was in over my head.

Half the crowd leaned forward and I knew they had their own versions of the same question. Theirs might be about curfew, parties, handing over car keys, or searching through text messages, Internet histories or their kid's room. But I knew their questions all came down to the same thing. *How could they know when to withhold freedom and when to give it; and could they do it without losing their kids in the process?*

Everything except the falling snow grew still. The dad was waiting, his eyes on mine, his question hanging between us. A beat passed and his words seemed to float downward, like so many indoor snowflakes that would melt if I let them hit the floor.

I wanted to be somewhere else finding comfort in a mug of hot chocolate, but everyone was staring so I tried to buy time.

"How old's your daughter?"

"Fourteen."

"And the guy, is he twenty-two and drives a panel van?"

Smiles. "No. He's sixteen and rides a bike."

"When you say bike, you mean Harley?"

"Schwinn."

"Tattoos?"

"Don't think so."

"You own a roll of duct tape, an extension cord and a power drill?"

"Yup."

"Does he know this?"

"No, but I could tell him."

He was being gracious because even as I made my lame jokes, I could feel they were minimizing the weight of his concern. The anxiety behind his smile made me realize all my talk and big picture observations hadn't been enough. He needed raw and practical answers that would show him exactly what to say when he sat face-to-face with the daughter he loved.

I fumbled an answer, and hoped some of what I said helped, but later, as I sat alone with my hot chocolate watching the storm, I couldn't shake the conviction I'd owed him more. That perhaps I owed everyone more.

So I decided to start listening to teenagers, and to their teachers and parents, in a new way, to find answers I'd missed before. I began to document the things I heard, and now, after years and thousands of conversations, the observations that follow are the result of that listening.

I now know what I'd say to that dad.

*   *   *

At first I was discouraged by the stories I heard. What I was learning seemed to complicate things more than help. Dominos were falling, but it felt like they were falling in the wrong direction.

I noticed two disturbing themes. *First, every teenager I talked to sincerely believed they were done on the inside, even though they clearly weren't, which meant they felt diminished when their freedom was limited. And second, they consistently said the adults setting limits didn't trust them.*

This told me the answer I was looking for would need to limit freedom in a way that left the teenager feeling respected *and* trusted, but this seemed impossible. It was a Catch-22 because limiting a teenager's freedom, by nature, proves we don't trust them yet.

The only answers I could think of all involved sedative-laced darts. "Quick, Honey, hand me the blowgun; he's almost to the end of the drive."

I was even more disheartened when I realized many of the teenagers confiding in me had rebelled *because* they didn't feel trusted.

A fifteen-year-old girl from Fossil Ridge High School in Colorado summed it up. Her eyes were down and her leg was bouncing to the rhythm of her angst as she explained she'd been grounded for coming home drunk. "My mom never trusted me, so I guess I just got tired of trying. I honestly never drank..." she looked up with the expression of a second-grader pleading with a teacher to believe her "...I really didn't, but she always thought I was lying, so I don't know..." she shrugged, "...I guess it just felt hopeless and I figured why not."

She sincerely believed she couldn't change the way her mother saw her, so she became a self-fulfilling prophecy. I'm not trusted, so why be trustworthy? And she shut her mom out.

It reminded me of what the Canadian dad said. "I'm afraid I'm pushing her away..."

As a father myself, I knew I needed to find a way to limit my kids' freedom without shaming them, and to do it in a way that they'd feel I was on their side and not their back.

*   *   *

As I continued to listen, I noticed something encouraging, and a new, more promising domino fell.

When I talked to students who felt the most hopeless – those who believed it was too late for them, that they'd screwed up to the point that nothing could repair their relationship with their parent, teacher or coach, that their life was irreparably ruined[3] – I noticed how powerful it was when I was able to give them even the smallest strategy to make things better.

It might be a new idea of how to approach the adult, or some little thing they could do to begin regaining trust (just a simple first step, nothing transformative) and their demeanor would change and they'd thank me profusely for making such a big difference. It amazed me. Many would tell me later the conversation had been a turning point in their life.

I began to see even the smallest glimmer of hope that change was possible, and that there was something they could do to influence their situation, took away their of feelings of helplessness.

That's when I realized the answer didn't have to give them total control over their freedom, just the sense they could influence it.

*   *   *

---

3 Anytime I discern a child is at risk, I use the trust they've invested in me to immediately connect them with an adult in their school or community. They almost always choose their favorite teacher.

There were other epiphanies along the way, but the final domino began to tip one evening after sunset when I was leaving Disneyland with my friends Frank and Liana.

Frank and I were sweaty because we'd been sprinting wildly through the crowds on Main Street pushing his two kids in hard plastic Goofy-shaped carts. The kids were too old for strollers, but too young to keep smiling through fourteen hours on their feet. With each swerve or near miss, their laughter was loud enough to make Mickey wish Walt had drawn him with smaller ears.

We burst through the exit, and were stopped in stunned silence by an unexpected horde of thousands of teenagers. It was obvious they were waiting for something, and I doubted it was a turn in the Goofy carts.

We learned it was Disney's all night celebration for high school seniors, called Gradnite, and there were more than twenty thousand of them. That's a lot of hormones, which might be the reason they call it "The Happiest Place on Earth."

Hundreds of wrinkle-free eyes stared blankly as we began to move into the parking lot. I hadn't noticed the silence between us till Frank said, "I don't know how good I'd feel about my kids going to Gradnite."

I assumed he meant in the future, you know, when they no longer needed the carts. I asked why, and he said, "It just seems like trouble, all those kids together all night."

"Well hopefully by the time they're eighteen they'll be ready for something like that."

And here's what I love about my friend. The next morning he walked me to my car and said, "What you said last night got me thinking."

"*I* said something that made *you* think?"

"I know. Surprising. But what you said about my kids being ready by the time they're eighteen."

"Yeah?"

"I think I've been doing too much for them."

"Like what?"

"Like when I help Christian with his homework, it usually ends up me doing it while he watches. Last night made me think that's probably not the best way to get him ready for the future."

I climbed into my car. "Unless, of course, you plan on living with him in his college dorm. Which could be fun."

He ignored me. "And most mornings Juliana asks me to pour cereal or toast a bagel or whatever, and I do it. But she's old enough to do it herself, and should probably be making her own bed too."

"If she can work an iPod, she can spread butter."

"Yeah. Wait. What?"

I just smiled and drove off. I like saying vague things to make him think I know more than he does.

His kids are now thirteen and sixteen, and Frank would tell you seeing all those teenagers at Gradnite changed his paradigm. He realized all the loving energy he was putting into being a dad would fall short if he didn't start thinking about *preparing*.

He'd figured out there's more to loving his kids well than being a Disneyland Dad. And he learned it in Walt's parking lot.

I like that.

*   *   *

We've all heard stories of teenagers who were great till they left for college, where it became clear they weren't prepared for all the freedom.

"He was such a good boy. Now he does crack."

"She was such a lovely teenager. Now she's a stripper."

None of us want that, but I noticed how common it is to think about preparing kids for their future in the same way many of us think about retirement. We know it's important, but it seems so far off and it's easy to be distracted by more immediate things like the latest smartphone or a more comfortable couch.

I kept coming back to the Canadian dad and how much he loved his daughter and wanted to be close to her. It hadn't been long since she was playing with stuffed animals, then overnight she wanted him to rely on her judgment about being alone with a boy.

A sixteen-year-old boy!

Talk about hormones.

So protecting her was a nonnegotiable, but I began to wonder if there was a way her desire for more freedom could be used to *prepare* her for that inevitable day when she *would* be alone with a boy she liked.

*   *   *

Everything since that night in Canada led me to see that *the answer lay in giving teenagers the chance to earn a measured amount of freedom now, with the hope of more to come, if they handled what they earned well.*

This gave shape to the following True Point. It's been refined and tested, used by teachers and families, including Linda,

Rob and Heather, and comes down to the three simple words Kristen and I have hanging on our kitchen wall.

"FREEDOM IS EARNED"

For years Kristen and I have lived our days to get to 8:00 p.m. That's bedtime for the three we have at home. It means we get to close the hall door and pretend we don't have kids for a while.

Bliss!

We've told them they have to be in bed by eight because research says they need ten to eleven hours per night at their age.[4] But the deeper reason is that's when we get to eat our secret stash of junk food, watch shows they aren't allowed to see, and set up the trapeze for wild monkey sex. [5]

Caleb recently turned thirteen and wanted a later bedtime. He also wanted more screen time because "gaming is good for his motor skills" (he likes killing things), and an iPhone so he can "use it for homework" (type "Megan Fox" into Google).

These are benign requests, but Kristen and I know the stakes are going to get higher as he gets older. Especially since the community we live in has lots of teenagers with easy access to alcohol and pot.

His natural and healthy desire for more freedom meant it was time to talk about our True Points.

I share the conversation we had because it's the best way I know to explain how this True Point works. (In a moment I'll tell you how it applies to that dad in Canada). It was

[4] http://sleepfoundation.org/sleep-topics/children-and-sleep/page/0%2C2/

[5] Okay, so there's no trapeze or monkey noises, but I'm betting you breezed right past the other footnotes and only looked at this one. It's what I'd have done. Shrug. Smile.

preventative with Caleb, but has been transformative for other families with teenagers who are already rebelling.

Our daughter, eleven-year-old Brooke, wanted to sit in on the conversation, and we thought it couldn't hurt. Their ages meant our examples needed to be simple.

I grabbed some paper and a sharpie and we all sat down at the kitchen table. I said we wanted to talk about a cool opportunity they'd get over the next few years, and Kristen said they could stop us any time with questions.

I started to draw.

When you were little, we put fences around you to keep you safe.

We put one around your play area outside to keep you safe from things like cars.

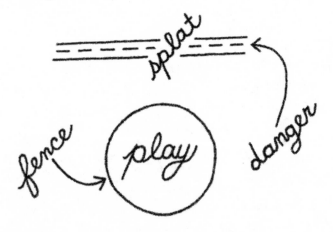

Then later, when you learned not to run into traffic, we took the fence away because you didn't need it anymore.

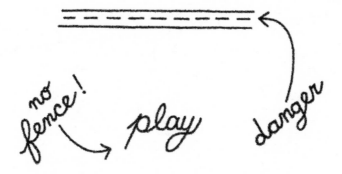

Even though that fence is gone, there are other invisible fences we put in your life to protect you. Like Caleb, remember in sixth grade when we found out you weren't doing all your homework, and we said you had to do it right after school before you did anything else? That fence protected you from failing classes, and taught you to have a better work ethic.

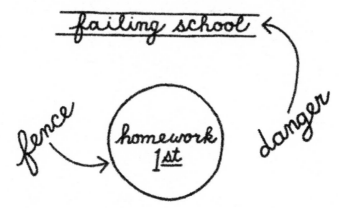

When we put that fence up we had to remind you about it every day, and sometimes you'd complain. That proved it was an important fence because without it your homework wouldn't get done.

But then, eventually you showed us you took the fence seriously, and did your homework well and without complaining, which showed us you were ready for more freedom. So we changed things and let you decide when to do your homework.

So here's the cool part. When you showed us you were ready for more freedom, we put a gate in the fence and opened it for you.

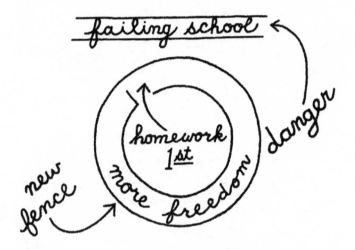

This is how we see every category of your life. *When you show us you can handle the freedom you already have, we promise there'll always be a gate that opens to more freedom.*

Our goal is the same as your goal. We can't wait for the day when there are no more fences. The sooner the better! So we're on your side cheering for more freedom.

We can't wait till you don't need a curfew, and we don't need to ask about homework or exams, or give you screen time or bedtime, or talk about respect. It would make our lives so much easier.

But here's the thing: when you guys go off to college we won't be around to put up fences, so our whole job now is to prepare you to be eighteen and handle everything without us, like laundry, studying, choosing friends, sleeping, dating, time, money, eating well, wearing deodorant.

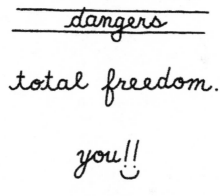

There will always be dangers, but the fences we put up now, and the gates you earn, will help you get ready to handle them on your own.

We promise as soon as you show us you're ready by your consistent behavior, we'll open a gate. Remember, even though we're in charge of the gates, getting them open is up to you.

Kristen took over.

"Caleb, you want a later bedtime and we're going to give it to you."

He smiled.

"Since you're a teenager now you only need nine hours,[6] but that's not why we're giving it to you. We're moving your bedtime from eight to nine because you've earned it by getting

---

[6] http://sleepfoundation.org/sleep-topics/children-and-sleep/page/0%2C2/

up on time every morning without being grumpy, and doing great in school.

"Also you can use the hour for extra screen time if you want. You've earned that since you've been getting your homework done without us having to bug you, and you haven't been asking to be on a screen every five minutes."

He was still smiling and sat a bit straighter. He was feeling proud, and that's something we want him to feel a lot.

Open gates create that feeling.

We also told him he could earn the right to have an iPhone when he started using his flip phone more responsibly, and saved enough to pay for half the iPhone and all the data charges. The next Saturday he went to our neighbor and negotiated a yard job and made $50 in five hours. He was proud of that too. And so were we.

Back at the table I wrote...

Freedom
is
Earned!

I asked Brooke to hang it on the kitchen wall above the note that says, "We are not the Kardashians" (we point to that anytime one of us is acting like we're the most important).

Kristen explained we were still in charge of setting values, and the amount of freedom they get depends on their behavior not their age. Brooke might earn a freedom before Caleb, even though he's older.

Brooke asked what she meant by values, so we explained they're the things we expect, like being honest or grateful or encouraging. We expect everyone to do chores well because our values are doing our best and serving others. Or we make you pay your brother five dollars if you call him a jerk, because one of our values is we don't call people names. (We discovered Brooke loves buying clothes with her money and losing cash hurts her, so it's a great consequence. Money is a privilege, and having it is a freedom she can lose. We've applied this to all the kids.)

My old friend Dolores was right: *Lectures don't work. Consequences do.*

Caleb said, "So you guys are the gatekeepers."

And I said "Yes, but call me Captain My Captain."

They laughed.

Kristen explained if they complain because we say they're not ready for a gate to open, they're proving they're not. Then she said the most important thing so far...

The Gates Swing Both Ways

If you earn a freedom, like a later bedtime, and your actions show you're not ready for it, it just means you have to go back through the gate. If we have to keep telling you it's time to turn off your light, or you're grumpy a lot, we'll know you weren't ready for 9:00 p.m.

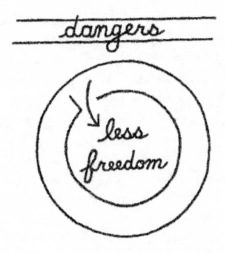

You'll make mistakes, we all do, but you get to keep the freedom you earn by showing us you're ready for it by your consistent behavior. If you lose a freedom, it won't be because we're grumpy or don't want you to have fun. It's because of something you've done.

*   *   *

Then we wrapped everything up by saying the most important sentence in this book.

If you break our trust, we'll give you every chance to regain it!

Those words are worth reading again if you have a moment. We'll come back to them in the next chapter, but before we move on, I want to tie up some loose ends.

*   *   *

What about that dad in Canada?

If I could go back to that snowy night I'd tell him it *is* possible to stay close to his daughter *and* protect her at the same time.

I'd remind him that how she'll end up valuing herself depends heavily on how she thinks he values her, and I believe their circumstances give him an amazing chance to show how much he does.

Then, with his permission I'd tell him what I'd say if she were my daughter, as an example of how he might approach things.

Something in his question suggested he was a single parent, so I'm going to speak from that perspective. I'm calling his daughter Brooke, since Kristen and I will probably have a similar conversation with our daughter in the next few years. I've given the boy she likes the name Scott. Kristen suggested this and I'm sure it has nothing to do with the fact her latest TV crush is Scott Foley. [7]

Here's how I'd begin...

*   *   *

Brooke, I know you like Scott a lot and he's really important to you. That means this whole thing's important to me too. I know you spend time together at school, and you're bummed I haven't thought you're ready for more than that, but I've been

---

[7]

thinking and have a plan for how you *can* be together with my full blessing.

If he's as great as you say, Scott won't mind any of this, since he already knows you're worth it.

Before I say more, I want to make you two promises. I promise I'll do my best to *never* embarrass you or him. In fact I've told your little brother if he embarrasses or teases you about Scott, I'll come down on him really hard.

And then I also promise as soon as you and Scott show me you're ready, I'll open gates. So I'm not saying you can't be with him, I'm just saying it has to happen one step at a time. And the good news is you have a lot of power to influence it.

For a first step, you can invite him over and do something fun and low pressure with us as a family. If it makes it easier, you can invite some other friends over the first couple times. You can decide what we do, but lets make it something easy on him where he doesn't feel pressure to make conversation, since hanging out with a girl's family can be pretty intimidating. I could make my famous tacos while we all watch a movie, or we could go to a hockey game, or whatever he's into.

I know if he likes you, which I'm sure he does, he'll do whatever it takes to spend time with you. Remember, he's the lucky one, so you should feel confident. As you know, guys like girls who are secure more than ones who act desperate or needy.

Then, after a while, depending on how things go, I'll open a gate that gives you the chance to hang out alone together here. Maybe he comes over for a BBQ, and after, we leave you alone to watch TV or play video games or just hang out.

Then, after a while of doing things like that, if it goes well, I'll do things like drop you guys off at a movie, or the mall, or wherever, then pick you up after a certain amount of time.

So you see how this works? It gives you both the chance to earn more freedom, and if you still like each other after a while, you'll get to hang out alone a ton, so long as you both keep honoring our values and this process.

Scott's going to have to earn gates too. So if he doesn't treat you well, or thinks hanging out with your family's lame, or is impolite or disingenuous in any way, the gates will open much slower, if at all.

You deserve to be with someone amazing, and all this will give us a chance to see what Scott's really like and how much he values you outside school.

At some point in all this, not yet, but sometime, once he feels more comfortable around me, I'm going talk to him to let him know you're the most important thing in my life, so how he treats you is important to me. I won't make it all heavy or intimidating, but I will be clear how he treats you matters, and how he respects us and this process has everything to do with how much time he gets to spend with you.

Remember, all our values are at play in this, and there are things that are nonnegotiable, like keeping your life balanced. This relationship can't become so consuming it dominates your time. I know you're crazy about him, but your schoolwork has to stay a priority, and so does spending time with the family, and your girlfriends, and things like that.

This whole thing is built on trust, so sneaking around this process, or doing things like texting when you're supposed to be asleep, or hiding anything, will show me you're not ready and gates will swing the other way. But I'm not worried 'cause I know how important this is to you, and I'm proud of you for being honest with me about how much you like him.

Also, you guys won't be allowed to be alone in your room with the door shut, or to be here or at his house when nobody's there. Not because I don't trust you. I just don't want Scott to be in a situation where he might get confusing messages about your standards and hurt your relationship by trying something that doesn't honor you.

Then the last thing before I hear what you think, sometime before you guys get total freedom, you and I are going to talk about sex, the things that lead up to it, and what your own standards are. We'll even talk about how you can talk to him about your standards.

If you guys aren't comfortable talking about touching each other, then you're not ready to touch each other. I don't want you getting hurt in that way, cause it can ruin a relationship really fast. And by the way, you having a conversation with Scott about your standards, when the time comes, is a significant way to show me you're ready for even more freedom.

I've got to be really honest; this whole thing is scary for me. Not because I don't trust you, but because you're growing up and aren't my little girl anymore. So you need to be patient with me in this process too. But I respect you, which is why I'm giving you this chance to earn freedom. I'm going to show how much I believe in you by how comfortable I make this process for Scott.

Also, if you make a mistake, I'll always give you the chance to regain my trust.

So what do you think about all this? Do you have any questions or is there anything you want to say?

(I think it's important he doesn't mention her age in this discussion. Saying things like "You're only fourteen" or "You're too young to know what's best" will make her feel prejudged and caged, as if there's nothing she can do to influence things. The most relevant things for her to hear are that she has the ability to prove her maturity by her actions, and he cherishes her.)

*   *   *

It's important to ask what she thinks. Even if she's mad because she wants more freedom, he needs to make her feel heard. This is more important than trying to change her mind when her emotions are running hot. It might be more productive to just listen, and then tell her he wants to think about what she said.

I've talked to many parents who end up in fights with their kids because they feel an urgency to react right away. I struggle with this same urge to solve things "now" in all my relationships, but I'm working on trying to remember *it's usually better to respond than react.*

It's scary to give a teenager a path to more independence, especially if they tend to make dumb choices. But if we don't, we risk pushing them into rebellion. If we never give them the chance to make mistakes and learn from them, they won't be prepared for the day they leave our care.

It's counterintuitive, but extremely important we give them chances to fail, and suffer, and get hurt.

The last thing I'd tell that dad, if I had a do-over, is to be strong and unapologetic about the fences he puts in place.

She'd rather disagree with him about certain fences than find him weak or inconsistent.

Just ask Heather.

*   *   *

So what did happen with Heather?

As it turns out, Linda and Rob followed Dolores' advice and sat Heather down and apologized for being inconsistent and forgetting their role. They said they understood why this frustrated her. Then they talked about fences and gates, and as expected, things went smoothly till one Friday they said she couldn't wear another revealing top. She stormed out yelling, "I don't care what you think!"

When she got home they'd taken away all her skimpy clothes. She yelled some more, and when they wouldn't give in she decided to run away. They didn't yell or chase or try her cell.

At almost midnight she called to ask if they'd come get her because she was sorry and her friend's family was weird and she didn't like being there. They didn't lecture, but said no; if she could run away on her own, she could get herself home.

I was especially proud of them for this, knowing how counterintuitive it was, and how contrary it was to their natural desire to nurture.

Then they added if she did come home, she couldn't come inside till she apologized for what she'd said and how she'd yelled before she left. And if she wanted to live under their roof, she'd have to live under their authority and values. If she wasn't willing, she should just stay at her friend's house, and wouldn't be allowed to come get any of the stuff they'd provided, like clothes and shoes. They also said they'd cancel her cell service since she didn't want to be under their care. They didn't negotiate or beg her to come home.

She screamed she hated them and hung up. It was a sleepless night, but in the late morning she rang the doorbell and apologized saying she'd live under their rules and asked if she could come home. They didn't lecture, they just hugged her and said *they'd give her every chance to regain their trust.*

There was some more, smaller testing, but things settled down once she saw where the fences were and understood she couldn't jump over them. They knew they had their daughter back when she told them she'd broken up with the boy at school because she wanted to be with someone more like Rob. They told her how proud they were.

She continues to test from time to time, they're trying to be as consistent as they can, and Rob is no longer jealous of the Stepford family down the street.

*   *   *

You can skip what follows and move on to our last chapter together if you like, but in case you're curious I wanted to address some important questions I'm often asked. Like how does all this help teachers? And should we search through text messages, Internet history or our kid's room? And if so, should we do it in secret, or in front of them?

*   *   *

For teachers.

As you know, teenagers get bored easily and love variety.

This is also true in class.

Every school has teachers who have given up on creative ways to engage students. They resort to lecture-filled class time in which students passively listen, because it's the simplest way to manage student behavior. Even though most of their words bounce off bored minds, they don't know how else to get through the material without losing control of the class.

I could never judge them for this, because if it weren't for Dolores, my own out-of-control students would have ended my teaching career.

It's almost impossible to offer creative options and variety in class when a few jerks are trying to ruin it for everyone, but I've discovered that fences and gates work well when coupled with the hope of earning a more fun, more varied and looser class experience.

For the Canadian dad it was the hope of alone time, for a teacher it would be things like less lecture and note taking, and more group work, learning games, independent time, fieldtrips, interacting with technology, movies, fun competitions with rewards like no homework or free food and so on.

The class gets to earn that variety by handling the current class experience with respect. It gives them a common goal, and when poor behavior of a classmate threatens the freedom they want, students are usually harder on each other than teachers are.

* * *

What about searching rooms?

If there's a specific reason to suspect a teenager is hiding something (not just a vague feeling, but some tangible warning sign like glassy eyes, or the sudden need to carry Visine, or a pattern of chewing fresh gum and avoiding being close to you when they walk in the door after being with friends, or cutting school, or a sudden change of friendship groups, or withdrawal from family, or uncharacteristic mood swings, and so on.) then it's very important to search their room.

However, because we tell them trust and respect are important, we also need to offer it to them, so I believe we should not search behind their backs. There really is no need to.

If there is a warning sign, we should tell them we want to talk to them in private in their room. When we get there, we should explain exactly what we've noticed that has us concerned, then explain we want them to stay with us while we look through everything in their room.

We might say, "I don't expect to find anything, but I need to make sure there isn't something you need help with but don't know how to ask."

They probably won't hug us and say, "Thank you for helping me navigate this difficult and pressured stage in my development whilst my frontal lobe continues its growth!" But if we have a good reason to search, at least it will make sense to them. If they throw a fit, it might be because they're hiding something, and we should not back down.

I believe they deserve the respect of being asked, "Is there anything you want to tell me before I start looking?"

Then we should do a good search, looking for things taped to the back of drawers or under furniture, or in pockets of clothes they seldom wear, in every pocket in their backpack, in all their shoes, under their mattress including stripping their bed and so on.

If we don't find anything, I think it's important to remake the bed and explain that this parenting thing is hard because we hear lots of stories about great kids who get sucked into dangerous things, and we're doing our best and hope they understand why we searched. They might be angry for a while, but if we're consistently giving them chances to earn freedom, and actually opening gates when they do, they will understand we're doing our best to be on their side. It's okay if they feel angry, but not okay for them to yell or be disrespectful in any other way. It's important to remember, they want to respect us more than like us, so we can't compromise on disrespect.

If we do find something and they say, "It's not mine, I'm just holding it for a friend" I believe we should explain they're responsible for all their choices. The consequences of holding it for a friend are the same as if it were their own.

* * *

What about text messages and Internet history?

Teenagers should know we expect full access to everything on their computer and devices. The difference between the Internet and searching their room is this: there would only be something dangerous in their room if they chose to bring it in and hide it themselves. However, online there are dangerous people and influences actively and aggressively pursuing them and seeking entrance into their lives.

We should explain that, like them, we're grateful for the Internet and the convenience of texting and so forth, but the reasons we expect to have access to their online life are the same reasons we lock the house at night. Part of our job is to protect our family from online predators who are pursuing teenagers and preteens, with the desire to seduce, coerce and offer addictive and destructive images.

This is a nonnegotiable in our family. Cyberspace is a privilege, not a right, and if they don't give us total access, they don't get a computer, phone or device.

There are other ways we honor their privacy. They can talk on the phone and we won't listen. They can spend time with friends, and we won't follow them around the mall or insist on being included in their sleepovers. But as anyone who's ever been hacked knows, there's no such thing as total privacy in cyberspace, so online is not the place to expect it from us.

Kristen and I have told our kids they can earn more freedom online, just like in every other area of their lives. For example, as they earn it, they won't have to ask permission to follow someone on Instagram, or to sign up for the latest social media craze. But even as this freedom grows, we will continue to expect to know all their passwords so we can randomly check on this part of their life, for the same reasons we will keep locking the house at night.

*   *   *

While we need to be committed to keeping kids safe, there are some things we should never protect them from. Which leads us into the arms of our final chapter.

15

They Need a Safe Place to Suffer

Nobody liked Eddie Ribaldi. He was mean and the only kid in seventh grade without friends.

What amazed me most was no one ever made fun of his hands. They were huge. Picture Popeye without the anchor tattoos. They fascinated me and I marveled whenever he picked up a pencil or turned a page.

I never guessed one day they would hold the power to ruin my life.

*   *   *

It would have been a normal day if I hadn't slipped the knife into my pocket.

"Probably won't even show anyone," I thought, as I climbed into the backseat of my mom's car for the second day of eighth grade.

It was exciting to feel the weight of it hidden in my jeans.

But then, as we pulled to the curb and I scrambled out, the first pangs of regret mingled with my fun. I realized if a teacher discovered the knife I'd be in major trouble. They'd consider it a weapon and I'd be suspended. Maybe even expelled.

During first period I fumbled with it in my pocket till Dawn, the cute girl, noticed and I didn't want her to think I was doing something else in there. Then in second period, the older slightly hunchbacked substitute announced she was taking us outside for free time on the playground.

My buddies were next to me as we walked into the sunshine and I couldn't resist. "Want to know what's in my pocket?"

Sometimes testosterone is like a pill that makes boys dumb.

They followed me to the back corner by the fence and adrenaline pushed aside my nerves for the moment. I pulled it out and flicked it open. Sun glinted off steel.

I'd never chanced such punishment. No one in my family had. My older siblings would never have risked offending my parents' values and authority with such blatant disregard, but I was drunk with the power of it.

"Let's play chicken." The words were out of my mouth before I knew they were mine. We started throwing the knife, trying to stick it in the dirt near each other's feet without flinching.

And then within a dozen thumps of my pulse, both the knife and the situation were out of my control. More boys were drawn to the action and it became a feeding frenzy. I was teetering on the edge of panic but loved being at the center of it all.

I was the ringleader. An outlaw. Invincible.

Wrong.

My thirteen-year-old world hit the fan when the friendless Eddie Ribaldi grabbed my knife in one of his oversized hands and ran toward the building shouting, "Tyler's got a knife, Tyler's got a knife!"

Edward Chubby Hands!

My jaw dropped in fear and I took off after him. As I did, clarity forced her way into my unfinished brain. "Hey Stupid!

A knife's a dangerous thing when you throw it around a playground. Kids can get hurt. That's why it's illegal!"

I knew these things, but hadn't thought it would come to this.

No fool ever does.

Primal instinct kicked in as I chased him onto the blacktop, knowing I had to catch him before he reached the building. Desperation pounded in my head and he was just an arms length away now. I strained for the back of his shirt, but my fingertips only grazed the smiley face logo staring back at me.

The attempt cost me a stride.

My legs were longer and my motivation stronger so I caught up again. I leaned forward, almost too far this time, nearly falling as he darted to the left. Smaller kids scattered and his shouts became screams. "Tyler's got a knife!"

The panic moved to my throat and the logo mocked me as it rocked from side to side.

Just a few more strides.

Now!

I threw myself at his heels as we crossed the painted home plate of the kickball diamond. As we fell, both my jeans and the skin on my knees tore as they met blacktop. Gravel ground into flesh.

I didn't notice the pain till later because I was focused on my knife as it fell at the feet of Miss Castillo, the sour-faced, nature-loving art teacher. We called her, "Miss Hug-A-Tree-O."

Oh God please, anyone but her! Everyone knew she was mean and weird. She'd never been married even though she was totally old, like twenty-six or something. She liked trees and stuff, and every day wore a huge peace sign around her neck, swinging against tie-dye. She hated war and violence, which is why I suspected I wouldn't be getting extra credit in art for tackling the school outcast to the pavement while he ran for his life with my open knife in his hand.

The expression on her face verified my suspicion.

She snatched up the knife and caught my arm. I knew where she was dragging me, but the principal's office scared me less than knowing at some point I'd have to walk into the kitchen of my own home.

My parents were big on consequences and trust, so I knew my life had come to irrevocable ruin. I felt utterly alone. Before the day was done, I knew the ones I needed most, my family, would turn their backs and things would never be the same.

The fear of rejection is always the first lie of childhood failure.

I found myself walking toward my house at 11:30 in the morning after being suspended from eighth grade. I'd been kicked out. Banished. Deemed unfit to be in the presence of other kids.

Cute Dawn had seen me crying in the office, so I knew by now my weakness would be the talk of the cafeteria. I also knew that in the house up ahead, I was about to face parents who'd regret having me.

Both my rock and hard place had a street address.

I opened the back kitchen door like some gnat drawn to flame. My mom was on the phone with the principal when I stepped inside. The timing sucked. She had no time to reflect or ask herself what Jesus would do. Her youngest had brought a weapon to school, was standing in front of her, she'd just found out, and it wasn't even noon. Her particular shade of red warned me what was coming wouldn't involve milk and cookies.

She ended her lecture through gritted teeth. "Go to your room and wait till your father gets home."

My fear started to throb. The worst was yet to come. No one messed with my dad.

6:00 p.m. crept up to the house like a dark shadow, full of menace. I heard it arrive with the opening and closing of the garage door. He was home. His hands were powerful, and they were coming for me. I began to sweat as I heard him ascend the stairs.

He'd never lost control or raised his hand to me in anger, but my mind conjured nightmares.

I listened at my door. Was that a chain he was dragging? I heard the muffled sounds of his conspiratorial conversation with my mom, and then he walked up to the other side of the final barrier between us. He just stood there. I could hear him breathing. I shrank back to the corner by my bed.

His waiting was worse than his coming.

Fear toppled reality as I pictured his fist clenched around the handle of the machete he'd brought back from his business trip to the Amazon.

An eye for an eye. A blade for a blade.

The pocket door slid open and my lungs lost the ability to exhale. I didn't move and for a moment couldn't look. He stared till I did, then without speaking, unfurled one of his python-like fingers and motioned me to follow.

As he turned I saw no chain or machete, just car keys. My heart sank. I'd heard about kids who were sent away and wondered if he was taking me to one of those "camps" for troubled juveniles who are no longer welcome at home.

I felt frantic and wanted to run, but where? And for the first time in my life, but not the last, shame squeezed in to poison me.

All safety was gone.

Dead boy walking.

When we got to the garage he opened the front passenger door and motioned me in. He went around, opened the driver's door and tossed the keys on the seat next to me. It was then I realized he hadn't opened the garage door, and the dreadful thought exploded in my brain.

Death by asphyxiation!

But then he bent his huge frame into the car and sat beside me. Shoulder to shoulder. He closed his door and stared at the wall in front of us and said nothing. You could have heard a drop of sweat hit the vinyl upholstery. When he turned to face me, I sort of flinched.

Here it comes. I was about to be banished, sent away, given proof I'd outpushed every boundary of his patience.

It's been over forty years since that moment, and I can still remember the pacing of each word.

"*Before you tell me what happened today, I want you to know I love you no matter what you do. No mistake you've ever made, or ever will make, could change that.*"

Huh? Wow! What just happened?

Brain bewildered.

Breathing again.

He's not going to kill, dismember or discard me? I'm not going to have to do everyone's chores?

A brief pause. I looked at the wall.

I looked back at him. He was still looking at me.

His eyes smiled.

I smiled. Sort of.

As I remember that moment now, I'm struck by something significant. Though I didn't know it at the time, and I don't want to overplay this, his words had formed the two most profound sentences I would ever hear.

They taught me I was safe, in spite of being flawed.

Remember Moema, whose little brother tragically drowned in that aqueduct? Home was *not* a safe place for her because her mom never admitted her own mistakes, and reacted to even the smallest of Moema's as if they were terminal.

Her mom helps me understand what I shouldn't do. My dad was teaching me what I should.

We all need somewhere to run when we fail, and my dad showed me it was safe to run to him. He came right out and put it into words. He didn't assume I knew his love was unconditional. And he called what I'd done a "mistake."

There's a quality of hope to that word. It meant I'd *done* something stupid, but not that I *was* something stupid. It meant he didn't define me or write me off or recategorize me because of it, and he didn't shame me or ask how he could ever trust me again.

But he did ask me to explain what happened at school. And then he listened. Without interrupting. Not even once.

One of the purest forms of love is to do the work necessary to truly listen to someone. Fully engaged listening is unusual and extremely difficult because it takes strenuous effort to extend our total attention. It requires discipline to stop all multitasking, both physical and mental, and to set aside our prejudices and the typical self-focus of our minds, in order to completely concentrate on hearing the other person with empathy.

Most of the listening we do is selective. We skim across the surface of what's being said like a rock skipping on a pond. We need to skim most of the time for the sake of survival. It would be exhausting and impossible to completely focus every time someone says something. We wouldn't get anything done, and frankly, life would be pretty boring since most of what people say isn't all that interesting.

But as you know, there are times when love requires that we do the work to truly listen. The problem is a lot of these important moments come when there's strong emotion floating around. Like when your kid just got suspended.

There are times I know I need to focus my energy to listen to my wife or one of my kids, but in heated moments everything inside me wants to walk out the door. And when I stay, my tendency is to be a selfish listener; just waiting till the other person finishes their point so I can make mine. Or even worse, not waiting, but interrupting.

There is no more effective way to diminish another person, to show we don't esteem them, than to ignore them – and interrupting is just a more aggressive form of ignoring.

When I first started asking teenagers what bothered them most about adults, I expected to hear "Too strict" or "Hypocritical." But through the years, regardless of demographics, the top answer by far has been, "They don't listen." [8]

My dad didn't always listen fully, and I don't blame him. In fact I remember many times he told me to stop yammering on about nothing. But *his listening in that garage, in that important*

---

[8] I'm indebted to M. Scott Peck for his discussion of love and listening in his timeless work, The Road Less Traveled. (Section Title: The Work of Attention.) I think if we were all to read the first half of his book, it would save a lot of pain.

moment in my life, was an act love! It showed he valued me, and I never doubted that fact again.

When I was done talking I felt nervous because he didn't rush in to respond. I remember wondering if I'd made things worse.

"So you're not mad?"

"No, I'm pretty mad."

"So how come you're not yelling?"

"Do I ever yell?"

"Just that time Barry said, 'I'm not doing it; that's Mom's job.'"

He smiled, "I forgot about that."

"That was cool! I liked it when you yelled at him."

"I'm sure you did. But I brought you out here to tell you a story that might help you understand why I'm not yelling now."

"Is it about you walking to school in the snow?"

"Nope."

"Okay then."

"I know you didn't spend a lot of time with your grandma, because she lived in England, but she could be pretty negative, and when I was almost ten, two of my friends invited me to go to the municipal baths after school."

"That's creepy!"

"What?"

"They wanted to take a bath with you!"

"No, that's what they call indoor community pools in England."

"That's weird."

"No, England just has a different culture."

"Still, they should know what a bath is."

Sigh. "The point is I'd never been in a pool before and I was pretty excited."

"Never? Did you live in the ghetto?"

"Sort of. Above a fish market. Just let me tell the story."

"Okay."

"So there were two pools, and one was for kids. I remember being amazed at the smell of the air and water and that the huge windows were fogged up. It was a new world to me."

"Can I ask a question?"

Exhale. "Sure."

"Does this have to do with me getting suspended?"

"Yes."

"Can I have my knife back?"

Another sigh. "Please just let me tell the story."

"Sorry."

"So my friends ran ahead and jumped into the kid's pool. I didn't know it was shallow because they tucked up their legs to make splashes."

"Cannonballs."

"Yup. So when I jumped in, because I didn't know what I was doing, I landed with my legs strait and my knees locked. When I hit the bottom I heard this popping sound, and pain exploded in my back. It ran down both legs and I couldn't breathe. Years later a doctor said one of my vertebrae had been pushed out of place, and I'd ruptured two discs."

"What's a vertebrae again?"

"Do you listen in school?"

"Mostly I just stare at Dawn."

"Who?"

"Dawn. She's crazy pretty! She has way cool hair and..."

He held up his hand and took another breath. "Vertebrae are those bones down the middle of your back, and your spinal cord runs through them. It's where most of your nerves are. Anyway, you know how my back hurts all the time?"

"Yeah."

"Well the doctors say when I landed in that pool, my spinal cord was bent and got squeezed in two places."

"You shouldn't have jumped in like that."

"Thank you, I know that now."

"I'm glad I never did something like that."

"Me too. So anyway, I just sort of rolled out of the water and lay on my side for a while. It took time before I could breathe, and eventually the pain settled enough so I could walk home. The whole time I was afraid because I knew my mom was going to yell at me."

"Weren't you supposed to go swimming?"

"No, she knew I was going, but she criticized me anytime I did something she thought was dumb. She yelled a lot."

"But I don't get it. Why couldn't the doctor fix your back?"

"Well, that's why I'm telling you this story. I never went to the doctor back then because I never told my mom what happened. I couldn't face her."

"Do you think we could afford one of those above-ground pools?"

He closed his eyes for a second and drew a long breath. "I told you this story because when your mom and I started having kids, I decided I never wanted any of you to feel the way I did that day. I just want you to feel like you can come home and be honest, even when you make a mistake."

"So you're saying since Grandma was mean to you, I'm not in

trouble for getting suspended?"

"No, you're in a lot of trouble, which we'll talk about with Mom when we go inside. But first, I wanted you to know even though you did this thing today, I still love you and you can always come to me no matter what. Okay?"

"Okay."

"So you understand?"

"Yeah."

"Good."

We both looked at the wall, and when I looked back at him he was smiling, and I watched him for a moment.

"Thanks for not yelling at me."

He seemed to be focused on something far away, and I thought he hadn't heard. But then, still smiling and without turning his head, he said a distracted, "You're welcome."

It seems to me now that redemption has a way of folding itself back over time, so the act of giving me grace in that car was allowing the child he'd been to receive that same grace somewhere in his past.

We sat together in silence for a while and it felt comfortable.

Then I said, "So I have a question."

"What's that?"

"Does this mean I get my knife back?"

"Don't push it, Son."

"Mom says I have to apologize to Eddie. Do I?"

"What do you think?"

"Yeah, I know."

Another pause.

"You should see Eddie's hands. They're bigger than yours! Sometimes I just stare!"

He sighed again. I figured it was because his back was hurting. Another moment, then, "Dad?"

"Yeah?"

"If you love me so much, how come I don't get my knife back?"

He shook his head, got out of the car and motioned me to follow.

*   *   *

We went inside and talked to my mom about my consequences. I don't remember all the specifics, but they included apologizing to the principal, to Eddie *and* to Eddie's mom. I didn't know why I needed to say anything to her but I kept quiet about it since I was curious to see her hands.

The big consequence was I had to give half the money in my savings to charity. This, my parents said, would teach me it costs a lot when we break the law.

That one hurt because I'd saved $112 toward the ten-speed bike of my dreams. I still remember the amount because I'd earned the money delivering newspapers seven days a week to homes up and down the steep hills where we lived. Carrying that bag loaded with papers was heavy and it paid only $3.50 a week, so losing $56 set me back a lot. It also guaranteed I'd never bring another knife to school.

Looking back it impresses me my parents added to the punishment the school gave. *They believed suffering, when it's the result of a mistake, is a gift.*

The strength of their decision was an act of love not only because it helped me learn, but also because it proved there was someone over me who was strong, which met my need to feel safe.

*   *   *

Last September I stood in a high school parking lot in Corona, California, till about 11:00 p.m. talking to a mom and dad about their fifteen-year-old son. They'd moved from Iran eight months earlier, and their son loved it here and had made lots of friends. The problem was they'd found marijuana in his room three different times.

I asked what they'd done the first time and they said they'd flushed it, then lectured him saying they'd send him back to Iran to live with his uncle if they ever found anything like that again.

No consequence, just a threat.

I asked why they hadn't followed through the second time, and Mom said she thought sending him to Iran was too harsh a punishment, even though it had been her idea, and Dad said he didn't want their son to get bitter. So instead they tried to ground him (restrict his freedom), but he didn't respect that either and kept coming and going whenever he wanted.

One broken window had been left unrepaired; now all the windows were being broken.

I felt compassion for them because they'd lost control and didn't know what to do. Being a parent can empty us sometimes.

They wanted to be a safe place for him, but were having a hard time seeing that for them to be a truly safe place their love also needed to provide for, or even create, the experience of suffering in his life.

Homes and classrooms need to be forgiving places that offer every chance for trust to be rebuilt, but they also need to be places where consequences are consistent and strong.

This leads to the second True Point...which also hangs on our kitchen wall at home.

"THIS IS A SAFE PLACE TO REAP WHAT WE SOW"

They said they'd thought of turning off their son's cell service but hadn't because it would inconvenience their lives, as well as his. They admitted it would be more inconvenient if he was arrested for drug possession, but didn't know what to do since he wasn't listening anymore.

I empathized with their son saying how scary it would be to walk into a large high school in a new culture. His whole life had changed and he needed to feel accepted and safe. It's no wonder he'd turned to pot smokers, since they're often the most welcoming people at school, especially if you can get pot.

I told them what Linda and Rob said to Heather when she ran away (that she couldn't live under their roof unless she lived under their authority), and I could see the fear in their exchanged glances.

"Are you afraid he'd just leave, and you'd lose him for good?"

They both nodded. Their eyes were full. Their fear was making them feel helpless and stuck. Their intuition had convinced them giving consequences would push him away forever, and that thought overwhelmed them.

I didn't know if their fear would allow them to hear it, but I told them the best way to become close to him again was to go against their intuition and win his respect by taking a firm stand. If there weren't consequences, nothing would change and they'd just be funding his rebellion while he grew to resent them even more for seeming weak.

It was getting late so I told them one last two-minute story about a dad I respected because when his son punched a kid at school and got suspended, he went and asked the principal if there was something extra they could add to the suspension. He said he wanted it to be something his son would hate so he'd learn not to punch people.

He loved his son very much and when the suspension was over, every Friday afternoon they made his son clean the locker room toilets, floors and benches where the boys put their naked butts. The dad said it wasn't fun watching his son suffer, but he knew if his boy didn't learn the lesson now, he'd end up suffering much more if he punched someone when he was twenty-five.

In this way, early suffering is less painful suffering, and therefore more loving.

Before we left the parking lot they asked some more questions and said I'd given them lots to think about. In hindsight I think I may have overloaded them by saying too much too quickly. I do that sometimes.

Their hearts were full and they were still adjusting to a new culture themselves, so I encouraged them to make an appointment with one of the school counselors soon.

They thanked me again, several times, then the dad hugged me and his wife nodded her goodbye, and as we turned to head for our cars I thought what a strange and daunting thing it is to have strangers confess their secrets and ask for advice.

I paused by my car door and waved as they pulled toward the exit. They waved back and I thought of some other things teenagers have taught me I wished I'd said. I was tempted to run and tap on their window so I could tell them, but I didn't because I knew I'd said enough for one night.

I have that same feeling now for you and me and this little book.

*　　*　　*

I was tired as I drove home, but left the radio off to allow my mind to drift to the place it often goes after I talk to someone in pain.

It takes me back many years to the months when I was homeless and full of shame, and I find myself once again standing mid-span on the Golden Gate Bridge. It's nighttime and the fog is swirling around me as the wind drowns out the sound of the cars and trucks speeding past at my back. I feel the railing, smooth and icy, under my palms, and the skin on my face is numb from the cold. The wind is blowing snot and tears back along my cheeks and into my ears, but I hardly notice because of the hollowness in my chest. I'm trying to find a way to stop all the pain, but know I can't without scarring my sons. I feel hopeless and alone. Inside is only darkness.

It may sound strange, but I cherish that memory now because when I think of it a beautiful thing happens...

I remember there's always hope.

*　　*　　*

I want to thank you.

I know I'll write to you again, but before we go I want to

thank you for allowing me the indulgence of ending this book with a lesson from my dad, rather than from what 4 million teenagers taught me. I could have told dozens of stories that corroborate the importance of giving them a safe place to reap what they sow, but I wanted to honor my dad because he passed away while I was writing to you. He died during the weeks I was working on chapter six, about Sister Catherine and how Keiko's parents never told her they were proud of her (They Need to Hear the Words).

He was ninety-two, and in the difficult moments I still find myself wishing I could call him to talk about how much I miss my dad.

About a year before he died he called and said, "Mom and I are grateful for the comfy chairs you and your sisters and brother gave us."

He was talking about the chairs some elderly people need with motors that push the seat up and forward to help them into their walkers.

He said, "I have an ancient old man's body but I still feel twenty-three inside, so I don't know what I'd do if I was stuck sitting in one place all day. I don't want to sound ungrateful, but I'm wondering do you think they make loveseats that do the same thing?"

I asked why. He paused then said, "I just miss holding Mom's hand."

They'd been married sixty-seven years.

In the end it was the weakness in his back that took him. He reached across his bed to close the blinds, and something snapped. It turned out to be two vertebrae. The pain was immediate and within two weeks he was gone.

I've often wondered if his mom had been a safer place, and he hadn't had to hide his pain, if he'd still be with us today.

The last time I heard his voice was from the hospice room and bed where he would die the following morning. (In fact that same room and bed were where my mom would pass away eighteen months later. Just two months ago, as I write to you now. You would have loved her; everyone did.)

I don't think it was a coincidence that different hospice workers unknowingly put my Mom in the same room and bed where my dad had been a year and a half earlier. There was something about the quality of my parents' love that makes me believe my dad was waiting there to show my mom the way, and the instant she let go of her last breath he reached out and took her hand.

His voice was weak when we said goodbye. He could only muster two phrases, separated by a long slow breath.

"I love you my son..."

Pause.

"...I'm proud of you."

Sister Catherine was right. We do need to hear those words.

To Spencer Bement

If there has been any beauty in the telling of these stories, it's because of all you've taught me about writing. I am forever your apprentice.

Thank you for editing this book. For the hundreds of hours you spent pouring over each syllable of this manuscript, in an attempt to teach a speaker how to tell stories in written form. As you've taught me, writing is a different art than speaking, just as painting is different than singing, and though I still have much to learn, you've given me tools to grow.

Your name deserves to be on the cover of this book as much as mine, but then I'd have to give you more money, and I don't want to do that. So I hope these words of thanks are more valuable to you than any amount of cash. No seriously, I really hope they are because they're all you're getting.

We'd love to know what you think about this book.
Please drop us a note at:
feedback@BiteSizedWisdom.com

To book speaking engagements or make bulk book orders contact:
info@bitesizedwisdom.com

For more information about the author, please go to
BiteSizedWisdom.com

Thank You

Thank you Spencer and Paul, for loving me as you've grown into men, for continuing to invite me into your story, and for being so darn fun. I love you and am proud of you! And to Samantha for marrying Paul and making us all happier and richer.

To Kristen, my heart, for making my story complete, and for sharing Caleb, Brooke and Jakie with me. You're an incredible mom. Seriously. Also for carrying the weight of my OCD and extreme introversion on your back, and for believing my stories are worth telling. You are home to me.

To Mom and Dad for teaching me that funny is good, and words are beautiful. I miss you. And to Barry, Jeanette and Daryl for loving your little brother even though I'm not normal.

To Frank Tate for helping me turn a clumsy idea into this book. Your guidance and wisdom is a gift. I don't know what I'd do without your friendship (#10).

To Donna Dunwoody for taking me in when I was young, broken, and stained. And for loving me enough to feed me, and to make me leave when it was time.

To Pooch and Autumn Claytor for being my best friends.

To Dighton Spooner for being so generous with your wisdom and braised beef short ribs. To David Hahn at Media Connect for believing in me. It kept me going when the writing got lonely. To Dr. Paul Lewanski, for the generosity of his time and his quote.

To David Letterman for making me laugh five nights a week since 1983, for teaching me the power of self-deprecation, and to be me, even if it breaks convention.

To Dean Koontz for making me fall in love with words again, to Stephen King for explaining I must be willing to murder my darlings, and to David Sedaris and John Steinbeck for proving storytelling is art.

To Trisha Thompson at Small Batch Books for showing me less is more. To Jason Kleist for the beautiful cover. To Todd Ford for making all this look like a book. To the very talented teenager Jenna Miller for the sketches. And to Paul and Debbie Naudé for the kind generosity of sharing their pool house when I needed to write in quiet.

And a special thank you to all of you who allowed me to use your story. Especially Laurie. Our boys have a great Mom.